THE HANDMAID OF PIETY

and other papers on
Charles Wesley's hymns

Edward Houghton

The Wesley Fellowship

Published by Quacks Books
in association with the Wesley Fellowship

British Library Cataloguing in Publication Data
Houghton, Edward 1992
The Handmaid of Piety and other papers
on Charles Wesley's hymns

ISBN 0 948333 11 1

Cardback £3.95 from booksellers,
supplied by publishers
Or £4.45 by post from:
Rev. G.H. Sutton, 46 Prince Road,
Oadby, Leicester, LE2 4SB
or
Rev. E. Houghton, 2 Norton Crescent,
Towcester, Northants, NN12 7DN

viii, 125pp

Printed by Quacks Printers, 7 Grape Lane, Petergate, York, YO1 2HU

FOREWORD

It is a long time since I have so much enjoyed a book as I have Edward Houghton's 'Handmaid of Piety'.

I first met Mr. Houghton in the early days of his and my ministry, and much more recently shared his colleagueship in committees of the new hymnbook, 'Hymns and Psalms'. Those days reminded me afresh very vividly of his love and knowledge of Wesley's hymns, and of his commitment to them. And now this new study brings this out and makes his knowledge and expertise available to all.

'Handmaid of Piety' is a series of papers rather than a connected study and it is really quite superlatively good. With unusual scholarship he places Wesley's work in its literary setting, relating it to the Augustan age and to Wordsworth's 'Lyrical Ballads' and its celebrated preface. But he points out, in more than one way, that Wesley's hymns are not only fine lyrics, and comparable with secular lyrics; they are primarily religious lyrics whose strength lies in their message as much as in their form. They are concerned with man's relationship to God his Saviour: 'His interest is *the evangelical experience*, which is our experience *of God*, as he comes to us in his Evangel, in Christ'; and Mr. Houghton tells us at the outset of his paper, quite bluntly, 'I cannot promise to interest anybody in Charles Wesley's hymns who is not interested in his religion.' It is worth saying.

Some of the papers are concerned with the nature of the hymns in general; but others deal with particular themes and even particular hymns. We all know 'Wrestling Jacob', even if we do not sing it often; it is just fifty years since Ernest Rattenbury issued his epoch-making 'Evangelical Doctrines of Charles Wesley's Hymns,' — I bought the volume on its appearance and revelled in it — but not even Rattenbury got to the root of 'Wrestling Jacob' as does Edward Houghton. That paper alone makes the volume worth getting. Another paper that struck me forcibly is 'On the Edge of Calvinism'; Wesley's anti-Calvinist hymns are known to all — 'For all, for all my Saviour died' — but we too easily forget how much of truth there is in Calvinism; after all, while 'Thy sovereign, everlasting love' is pure Charles Wesley, 'sovereign' is none the less a very Calvinist word; and this paper explores Charles Wesley's Calvinism most profoundly. I must refrain from continuing.

I have read the whole in typescript with pure joy; I shall look forward to rereading it in its published form. Edward Houghton has done Methodism, and indeed the Christian world, a memorable service, in reminding us, in short, of the very nature of evangelical religion.

OLIVER A. BECKERLEGGE

PREFACE

It was my beloved tutor Dr. Henry Bett who effectively introduced me to Charles Wesley, and also (alas, only in print) to Bernard Manning his brightest interpreter. These, Bett and Manning, have been my teachers, most of all in showing me the spirit of the hymns.

All my ministry these hymns have been my absorbing interest and occupation, but it is thanks to the enthusiasm and practical drive of my friend the Rev'd. Harry Sutton that my work now appears. He introduced me to Paul Taylor, secretary of the Wesley Fellowship, who issue this little book. He found me two typists, Avis Dawson and Margaret Taylor (Paul's wife), who painstakingly and freely made something of my manuscribble (with later help from Carol Wells, Penny Bennett and Susan Henshaw of my own churches). And it was Harry's idea to ask a foreword of another friend of mine, Dr. Oliver Beckerlegge, co-editor of the Oxford edition of John Wesley's definitive Methodist hymn-book of 1780. I am encouraged by his kind commendation, and even more grateful for his expert help in seeing it all through the press.

So I send this out, believing I have been so led and that God has opened up the way. But I did just wonder! Need we be conversant with names as disparate as William Wordsworth and Tobias Crisp (who was he?) before opening our hymn-books to these hymns? Thankfully, not! All anyone needs do is *use* them, along with the Bible they came from. But these studies have helped me for one do that, and may help some others. The hymns are what matter, and God's greater glory by them.

TOWCESTER
August 1992

REFERENCES

HP   *Hymns and Psalms,* 1983.

MHB *Methodist Hymn Book,* 1933.

WH   *("Wesley's Hymns"), A Collection of Hymns for the use of the People called Methodists,* 1780. Oxford ed'n, 1983, ed. Hildebrandt and Beckerlegge.

Rep Verse *Representative Verse of Charles Wesley,* F. Baker, 1962.

Works *The Poetical Works of John and Charles Wesley* — 13 vols. ed. G. Osborn, 1868-72.

(Quoted in this order of availability. I have not given all references to generally known hymns.)

TEXT

For purposes of these studies, I have kept strictly to the original texts of hymns, except for small modernisations of lettering and punctuation. This, even where there are accepted revised readings (mostly John's). Thus *How can a sinner know*, written in 6.6.6.6.8.6.8.6., accommodated by John to DSM (*WH* 93); this explains the unfamiliar length of a line quoted in Paper 2. I have not even removed occasional offending words like 'bowels', or the very occasional word that has suffered in modern usage ('Give me a lot of love' — *WH* 392, Papers 6 and 11). I have used what Charles actually wrote, and we can easily make the few necessary adjustments. Most of his verse is quite intelligible today.

CONTENTS

Contents

1. THE HANDMAID OF PIETY

John Wesley, in preface to his definitive Methodist hymn-book,[1] having claimed (with decent modesty) for 'some of the following verses the true spirit of poetry', goes on to insist that 'what is of infinitely more moment ... is the spirit of piety', and expresses the hope that 'all persons of real judgment will find *this* breathing through the whole Collection.' He is referring principally to his brother's hymns (the bulk of the book[2]), and is saying that, as poetry, they serve the greater end of piety — not mere poetry (if poetry is ever 'mere'), but poetry 'the handmaid of piety'. These hymns are about God, and most of them are prayer. Wordsworth was to define 'all good poetry' as 'the spontaneous overflow of powerful feelings',[3] and supremely the poetry of piety is this — the feeling for God, and its spontaneous expression in verse. I cannot promise to interest anybody in Charles Wesley's hymns who is not interested in his religion.

But the hymns *are* poetry, lyrical poetry in the Augustan age of English verse, when lyricism was at a low ebb. Not that the lyric ever quite dried up in that century. For what is this but lyrical? —

> Come, my mates, let us work
> And all hands to the fork,
> While the sun shines, our hay-cocks to make.
> So fine is the day,
> And so fragrant the hay,
> That the meadow's as blithe as the wake.

> Our voices let's raise
> In Phoebus's[4] praise;
> Inspired by so glorious a theme,
> Our musical words
> Shall be joined by the birds,
> And we'll dance to the tune of the stream[5]

— 'musical words', or lyric. Indeed, these of Christopher Smart's are actually a hymn of sorts, 'AN HYMN FOR THE HAYMAKERS', in a characteristic Wesley metre. Compare this, dating only a year later, 1749:

> How happy are they
> Who the Saviour obey,
> And have laid up their treasure above;
> Tongue cannot express
> The sweet comfort and peace
> Of a soul in its earliest love. (*MHB* 407)

1

The lyrical affinity is striking, the mood of simple happiness. And Roger Lonsdale's lively anthology of the century's verse gives other examples of 'the vigorous, humorous, idiosyncratic verse of authors, many of them anonymous, who felt impelled at least to try to describe with some immediacy and colloquial directness the changing world they lived in, often for anything but a polite readership.'[6] That it was not all bawdy the Haymakers' Hymn is some evidence; and the upholders of fidelity are represented by David Mallet's admonitory 'WILLIAM AND MARGARET', which also is lyrical:

> Her bloom was like the springing flower,
>   That sips the silver dew;
> The rose was budded in her cheek,
>   Just opening to the view.[7]

That is sheer music, in Pope's hey-day (1723).

All this must qualify somewhat Henry Bett's absolute assertion that 'for a period, say, from the death of Henry Vaughan to the youth of Robert Burns the lyrical note was never heard in these lands.'[8] But he was substantially right. The dominant poetry was not lyrical, and the other poetry, that often was, was little recognised. 'In fact, throughout the century there were poets oblivious of, or indifferent to, the inhibitions of polite taste: the success of that taste lay less in governing what was written than in influencing what would be allowed to survive.'[9] Effectively, the one known and accessible lyric-form was the hymn. George Sampson's conclusion stands: 'The poetic diction of Pope and his imitators was not the language of the eighteenth century. It was the *patois* of fashion, the temporary dialect of St. James's. To find the real language of the age, we must turn to the hymn-writers, who spoke the language of the people, who affected many more thousands than the fashionable writers ever reached, and maintained the simple sincerity of feeling, the natural association of object and description, which needed no discovery, but was already there for Wordsworth to use.'[10] Pope has his stout defenders: 'Enthusiasts for Watts or for the Wesleys do their subjects no service at all when they set them up in competition with the greatest poet of their age.'[11] But we need not argue. However great a poet he was, he was not a lyrical poet, so is not further relevant to this discussion. It is a simple fact that lyrical poetry was scarce during Pope's reign, and Wesley's verse has the added value of most things in short supply. Wordsworth was never to write a truer lyric than *Christ, whose glory fills the skies* or *O, disclose thy lovely face*, and these came fifty-eight years before *Lyrical Ballads*.[12] So early, Wesley used 'the real language of men in a state of vivid sensation' and wrote poetry that was 'the spontaneous overflow of powerful feelings'.[3]

But if, as word-artist, Wesley painted in the same fresh Spring colours that Wordsworth was to use, it was a very different Spring he depicted. '*Lyrical Ballads* was published as an experiment ... to ascertain, how far, by fitting to metrical arrangement a selection of the real language of men in a state of vivid sensation, that sort of pleasure and that quantity of pleasure may

2

be imparted, which a poet may rationally endeavour to impart'[3] — 'What is of infinitely more moment than the spirit of poetry is the spirit of piety. And I trust all persons of real judgment will find *this* breathing through the whole Collection. It is in this view chiefly that I would recommend it to every truly pious reader: as a means of raising or quickening the spirit of devotion, of confirming his faith, of enlivening his hope, and of kindling or increasing his love to God and man. When poetry thus keeps its place, as the handmaid of piety, it shall attain, not a poor perishable wreath, but a crown that fadeth not away.'[1] Wordsworth's springtime is the *Lyrical*, Wesley's the *Evangelical* Revival.

But Wesley's poetry as lyrical well compares with Wordsworth's. 'Poetry', declared the Lakeland poet, 'takes its origin from emotion recollected in tranquillity: the emotion is contemplated till, by a species of reaction, the tranquillity gradually disappears, and an emotion, kindred to that which was before the subject of contemplation, is gradually produced, and does itself actually exist in the mind'.[3] The classic illustration of this would be his own lines on the daffodils:

> For oft, when on my couch I lie
>   In vacant or in pensive mood,
> They flash upon that inward eye
>   Which is the bliss of solitude;
> And then my heart with pleasure fills,
> And dances with the daffodils.[13]

Thus does he 'see' again what he saw that day. But strictly, this is memory — 'recollected' but not the actual experience, a 'kindred' but not the identical emotion. In line with that analysis, he had already had the anticipatory frankness, earlier in the Preface, to admit that, while a poet 'describes and imitates passions, his employment is in some degree mechanical, compared with the power and freedom of real and substantial action and suffering.' Now that distinction generally holds for Wordsworth — he profoundly understood his own work. But it does not explain Wesley's greatest writing. Compare Wordsworth's celebrated lines,

> And I have felt
> A presence that disturbs me with the joy
> Of elevated thoughts...[14]

with this one line of Wesley's,

> My God, I know, I feel thee mine.   (*HP* 740)

'I have felt' — 'I feel' : the difference is immediacy.

Nothing can be more immediate than the presence of God, and Wesley writes in the heightened present of this experience:

3

I cannot see thy face, and live!
  Then let me see thy face and die:
Now, Lord, my gasping spirit receive;
  Give me on eagle's wings to fly,
With eagle's eye on thee to gaze,
And plunge into the glorious blaze.

The fulness of my great reward
  A blest eternity shall be,
But hast thou not *on earth* prepared
  Some better thing than this for me?
What, but one drop! one transient sight!
I want a sun, a sea of light.[15]

These two stanzas, with their 'direct simplicity' and 'imaginative boldness',[16] were Bett's supreme example of Wesley's lyricism. Other of his verse can be less highly imaginative but even more simple and direct:

Thou callest me to seek thy face —
  'Tis all I wish to seek,
To attend the whispers of thy grace,
  And hear thee inly speak.   (*HP* 542)

Note the second line with its falling cadences in three pairs of single-syllable words; and the fourth, with its monosyllabic build-up from line 3 to its climactic word, 'inly'. This is the natural simplicity of uncontrived great art, and again, it has come of immediate awareness of God.

Wesley's is the immediacy of feeling that characterises the most authentic utterances of evangelical religion. No Christian could imagine a man not in the felt presence of Christ producing:

Just and holy is thy name,
  I am all unrighteousness;
False, and full of sin I am,
  Thou art full of truth and grace.

'Charles Wesley wrote every one of his innumerable hymns' (or every one that matters, being many) 'as if he had never written another'[17] — *because* each is in present-time, newly happening as he writes:

Coming as at first I came,
  To take, and not bestow on thee:
Friend of sinners, spotless Lamb,
  Thy blood was shed for me.   (*HP* 729)

.   .   .   .   .

> Every moment, Lord, I want[18]
> The merit of thy death.   (*MHB* 459)

Thus is evangelical experience being constantly renewed as evangelical, a sinner's experience of present grace:

> My trespass is grown up to heaven,
>> But far above the skies
> In Christ abundantly forgiven
>> I see thy mercies rise.

John, no doubt wishing to safeguard the assurance that is every believer's right, made the first line into:

> My trespass was grown up to heaven.

That is how we will always sing it, and the difference is slight, for the last line keeps the whole in present-time:

> I see thy mercies rise.

But just something of vividness may have been lost, a window into his brother's heart. Charles always came as at first he came. Grace means the need now for grace, that a gracious God now supplies. It is this presentness of evangelical experience that stamps the hymns with reality. This hymn is about God being gracious actually now. A sentimental hymn might recall 'seasons beautiful and rare' (*MHB* 469). A far truer hymn might ask, out of a felt emptiness:

> Where is the blessedness I knew
> When first I saw the Lord?

The *great* hymn will have the grand immediacy of faith:

> By faith we know thee strong to save:
>> Save us, a present Saviour thou!
> Whate'er we hope, by faith we have,
>> Future and past subsisting now   (*HP* 662)

— 'a present Saviour', 'we have', 'now'.

No wonder Wesley is the most lyrical of hymnwriters! Hymn after hymn comes of his actual experience of God, even from the very presence of God:

> But art thou not already mine?
>> Answer, if mine thou art!
> Whisper within, thou love divine,
>> And cheer my doubting heart.   (*WH* 177)

.   .   .   .   .

5

Pity from thine eye let fall,
By a look my soul recall,
Now the stone to flesh convert,
Cast a look, and break my heart!   (*MHB* 358)

.   .   .   .   .

My prayer hath power with God; the grace
 Unspeakable I now receive;
Through faith I see thee face to face,
 I see thee face to face, and live!   (*HP* 434)

.   .   .   .   .

I every hour in jeopardy stand,
But thou art my power, and holdest my hand;
While yet I am calling, thy succour I feel,
It saves me from falling, or plucks me from hell   (*MHB* 502)

— while yet I am calling!

 These verses, and countless like them, are pure lyric, and Dr. Bett hardly overstated his case in claiming their uniqueness in the poetry of that day. True, Lonsdale has other examples of contemporary verse that is simple, direct, and in main character lyrical. But not lyrical like Wesley's! His is the poetry of piety, the believing wonder, the songs of God's evangel that the heart sings back to God:

  Celebrate the eternal God
   With harp and psaltery;
  Timbrels soft and cymbals loud
   In his high praise agree:
  Praise him every tuneful string,
   All the reach of heavenly art;
  All the power of music bring,
   The music of the heart.   (*HP* 55)

These hymns, the liturgy of the Evangelical Revival, are the supreme witness in our tongue to evangelical religion as being the most vibrant, living, moving thing in all our lives. Truly (and I am not talking about a denomination), 'Methodism was born in song'.[19]

NOTES

1. *A Collection of Hymns for the use of the People called Methodists*, 1780.
2. H. Bett's findings as to authorship (*The Hymns of Methodism,* ed 3, ch 3) would give Charles 90% — 472 of 525 hymns.
3. Preface to *Lyrical Ballads.*
4. Phoebus: the sun.
5. R. Lonsdale, *The New Oxford book of Eighteenth Century Verse*, 283.
6. Lonsdale, op cit, p xxxvii.
7. Lonsdale, op cit, 115.
8. Bett, op cit, p 12.
9. Lonsdale, op cit, p xxxvi.
10. G. Sampson, *The Century of Divine Songs* (Warton Lecture, 1943), in *Seven Essays*, p 231.
11. D. Davie, *Augustan Lyric,* p 17.
12. *Hymns and Sacred Poems* 1740.
13. *I wandered lonely as a cloud.*
14. TINTERN ABBEY.
15. *To thee, great God of love, I bow* (*WH* 275), from Ex 33:18-23. (Cp also *WH* 274; 86:4).
16. Bett, *The Spirit of Methodism*, p 177. (Also, *The Hymns of Methodism*, p 12).
17. Sampson, op cit, p 224.
18. 'Want' — Wesley's is preponderantly the older usage, 'be in want of', 'need' (*HP* 291:1; 422:1,2; 528:3; 680:2-4; cp 275:4; 558:1 — the noun. Even 'I want a sun, a sea of light' (quoted) is not mere desire, but deep need; similarly *MHB* 459:4; 563:5,6.
19. Preface to *MHB* 1933.

2. WHAT WE HAVE FELT

Wesley's hymns are hymns of faith, and that means the Bible account of faith, which always and only is faith in God, and in Christ as God. Thus to believe is no mere subjective happening, but is the response to revealed truth:

> Faith lends its realizing light,
>   The clouds disperse, the shadows fly,
> The Invisible appears in sight,
>   And God is seen by mortal eye. (*MHB* 662)

It is vague, then, and misleading, simply to label Wesley as an experimental hymn-writer. His interest is *the evangelical experience,* which is our experience *of God,* as he comes to us in his Evangel, in Christ. There is the Evangel before there is any evangelical experience, and there is God before there is any Evangel. Emotion is incidental to this experience (though a normal incidence), and even moral renewal is only consequent upon it (though its necessary consequence); *God* is essential to it. The value of these hymns depends on the truth of God. What they say would be true had Wesley never lived and they not been written; but not if Christ had never come.

Experience, for Wesley, is not the ground of faith, but truth is; that exists in its own right before any faith or experience of ours. Thus, what Christ *is for me* rests wholly on who Christ *is:*

> Thou the Father's only Son,
>   Pleased he ever is in thee;
> Just and holy thou alone,

then

> Full of grace and truth for me. (*WH* 187)

The complete misunderstanding of Wesley (and betraying a most unWesleyan general attitude to religion) would be to consult him *on* religion, but not on theology. If his theology falls, so does his religion — it is that sort of religion.

The heresy that mere feeling (or 'enthusiasm' on its eighteenth-century definition) is any substitute for Christian fact and truth has nothing to do with Wesley, nor yet the notion that these are determined by what we feel. But it is a very general assumption that Wesley's hymns are mainly about his Christian feelings. Thus Canon Adam Fox, when he declared that, in comparison with Watts (whose complementary genius we all recognise[1]), 'Wesley has more of a lyric touch but less substance.'[2] (Watts himself would not agree.)[3] Wesley at best is not touched but *infused* with the lyric spirit, (the qualification 'at best' would be needed for Wordsworth no less); and the *substance* of his hymns is the Christian confession of God. Much the same assessment of Wesley came from a very different quarter — Dr Martyn Lloyd-Jones, rather surprisingly, in the course of an authoritative address on *William Williams and Welsh Calvinistic Methodism*:[4] 'The hymns of William Williams are packed with theology and experience ... You get greatness... in Isaac Watts; you get the experimental side wonderfully in Charles Wesley. But in William Williams you get both at the same time.' As to Williams, no doubt — the Doctor knew his subject. But the same is precisely true of Wesley, who cannot be marginalised on some 'experimental side' of religion. His hymns are *theological and experimental* through and through. They are about

> What we ourselves have felt and seen, (*WH* 93 — *HP* 728)

and with confidence tell. But this is first what we have believed of Christ,

> That he for us hath died.

There follow four interrelated words: we 'feel his blood applied'. Which may strike us oddly today — it does appear rather an accident of words that 'applied' rhymes with 'died' (like notoriously 'love ... above' in hymns); and the precise expression is not scriptural.[5] But Wesley knows what he is saying — that the historic death of Christ means salvation for Christians now. His experience is grounded in the Christian confession: 'feel ... applied' (experience), 'his blood' (confession). The same:

> See there my Lord upon the tree!
> I hear, I feel, he died for me   (*HP* 226)

– faith ('I feel') comes of the Faith ('I hear'): faith comes of hearing, and hearing by the word of Christ.

Thus to equate faith with feeling is not to debase the former, but to elevate the latter. Wesley specifically means feeling *in a believer*, so faith defines it — the inner persuasion that the Gospel is true. But the word itself properly means more than we have it mean. Wordsworth explains what the English poets mean when they tell us they 'feel': 'You have given me praise for having reflected faithfully in my poems the feelings of human nature ... But a great poet ... ought, to a certain degree, to rectify men's feelings, to render their feeling more sane, pure, and permanent, in short, more consonant to nature, that is, to eternal nature, and the great moving spirit of things.'[6] Mercifully, his poetry is less tedious than his prose explanations, and here are famous lines to illustrate what he is trying to say:

> And I have *felt*[7]
> A presence that disturbs me with the joy
> Of elevated thoughts; a sense sublime
> Of something far more deeply interfused,
> Whose dwelling is the light of setting suns,
> And the round ocean and the living air,

> And the blue sky, and in the mind of man:
> A motion and a spirit, that impels
> All thinking things, all objects of all thought,
> And rolls through all things.[8]

'Feeling' is here the most fundamental process of *thought*, interpreting *reality* in terms of what is most rational and moral in us. Wordsworth's world of feeling has not come merely of his feeling it, but is a world he has entered upon,

> the mighty world
> Of eye, and ear — both what they half create,
> And what perceive; well pleased to recognise
> In nature and the language of the sense
> The anchor of my purest thoughts, the nurse,
> The guide, the guardian of my heart, and soul
> Of all my moral being.

All this is far enough away from Wesley — as far as near-pantheism or a philosophy of nature from evangelical religion. But the two have in common a *definition* of feeling as the profoundest apprehension of truth; with for Wesley this vital qualification, that the feeling is religious, and yet more explicitly *evangelical* feeling, since the felt truth is simply the truth of the Gospel, and concerning reality that is not half-created by sense-perception (or even by faith), but is wholly given by God in his word; so that

> The things unknown to feeble sense,
> Unseen by reason's glimmering ray,
> With strong, commanding evidence
> Their heavenly origin display. (*HP* 662)

There is an objectivity of revelation in all this, and it is the Holy Spirit who 'makes to us the Godhead known'. When by him we say, 'Jesus is Lord' (*I Co* 15:3),

> Then, only then, we *feel*[7]
> Our interest in his blood,
> And cry, with joy unspeakable,
> Thou art my Lord, my God!

This *feeling* is Wesley's full synonym for *faith,*

> the living faith
> Which whosoe'er receives
> The witness in himself he hath,
> And consciously believes. (*HP* 325)

It is a mistake, then, to talk of 'feeling' in Wesley as though it were a term of mere subjectivity. 'Wesley's appeal was not to the reason but to the intuition', declared Norman Nicholson, too easily, in a broadcast talk to mark the 250th anniversary of the poet's birth, citing:

Should know, should *feel*[7] my sins forgiven. (*HP* 706)

But the feeling is faith and is *sui generis* — not formal reasoning, certainly, but not intuition either, *other than* specifically the Christian's intuition that is faith. This is demonstrated by the story of the hymn, which its author told in his private journal — how he had gained full assurance of faith under the ministrations of two simple lay people, John Bray, 'a poor ignorant mechanic who knows nothing but Christ' (Wesley's description) and Mrs Musgrave, 'a weak, sinful creature' (her self-description), both in awe of Wesley as a minister of the Church. Not only had they little education (Bray could read), but no impression is given of any striking gifts of personality in either of them. It is not to be supposed that they did anything to quicken the poet's intuitive faculty. What they were used of God to convey was the new distinctive faculty of faith: 'I saw that by faith I stood; and the continual support of faith, which kept me from falling'. That was Whit Sunday, 1738, and on the Tuesday morning, 'At nine I began a hymn upon my conversion.' On Wednesday evening, 'Towards ten, my brother was brought in triumph by a troop of our friends, and declared, 'I believe!' We sang the hymn with great joy and parted with prayer.' It was from that hymn's opening line that the speaker took his title:

Where shall my WONDERING SOUL begin?

The wonder was a converted man's wonder, evangelical wonder, the feeling-tone of faith. He wondered because he believed, he never wondered himself into believing — as Blake, whom we are to come to, perhaps tried to do. Wesley's is the new poetry of faith.

That is why we cannot go on from Nicholson's discussion of this historic hymn to his general conclusion that its author was more a man of the nineteenth 'than of his own eighteenth century, a man of intuition, extravagance and imagination ... and he belonged, one might say, beside Coleridge and Blake rather than beside Pope and Watts.' As to poetry, nearer affinities might be found in the lyricism of Burns and Wordsworth. But all such matchings must be superficial, since they ignore, or cannot see, the *faith* that is the meaning of all Wesley's hymns. We have noted a common ground to Wesley and Wordsworth as poets — a serious apprehension of reality, with form always the very good servant of matter. What affinity, even so far, has Wesley with Blake? Indeed there was an earlier Blake, who wrote imaginatively before his poetry became imagination *per se*. Then he could be delightful, with childlike uncomplication in utter contrast to his own later complexity. For imagination that is perceptiveness, an image of the world around us, with lightness of touch and the originality of being simple, Wesley has nothing like THE ECHOING GREEN, THE LAMB, THE LITTLE BLACK BOY, and others. Blake, before he spoiled himself, was the poet for children and the child in us all. Wesley, whose hymns for children were generally a disaster, or not for children at all[9], can only suffer here in comparison. But it is the very different later Blake that Nicholson seems to have in mind — intuitive, extravagant, imaginative. Possibly this style of writing has actual attraction for some who prefer impressions to analysis and are happier not to be pinned down to a clear meaning. *And did those feet*, now immortalised in music, is that sort of thing, and certainly succeeds. But few have read the rest of MILTON, the long poem which opens with those lines, and it is patent if you try that he has now passed quite beyond 'the real language of men'[10] or the 'common sense' of words,[11] and so beyond any remote resemblance to Wordsworth or Wesley. Here is how *The Ghost of Abel* begins — his last published poem:

> What dost thou here, Elijah?
> Can a poet doubt the visions of Jehovah?   Nature
> has no outline,
> But imagination has. Nature has no tune,
> but imagination has.
> Nature has no supernatural, and dissolves:
> imagination is eternity.

These opaque lines express in character Blake's high doctrine of imagination, that has carried him beyond the main usefulness of words. Thereafter he was to concentrate on his futurist pictorial art, always his first love. *He certainly* is of the nineteenth century, 'a man of intuition, extravagance and imagination'; but not Wesley, who never wrote like that, or could have done.

Not that Wesley is without imagination or indeed that this can never go wrong:

> I rode on the sky
> (Freely justified I)
> Nor envied Elijah his seat;
> My soul mounted higher
> In a chariot of fire,
> And the moon it was under my feet. (*Works* iv, p 409[12])

(And we remember what the nursery rhyme cow did!) A seductive metre has led him on and away in a quite uncharacteristic flight of fancy, to the unscriptural union of scriptures not joined together by God.[13] But the extravagance is occasional and only verbal — it never really breaks the bounds of meaning, here the joy in believing, that so many of his hymns so much better express. With Blake, the extravagance is conceptual — his stock-in-trade, his intended art. Wesley's poetry has imagination, but is never merely that and for its own sake. Its basis is always experience, often imaginatively expressed; and usually it rings true:

Great God, to me the sight afford
  To him of old allowed,
And let my faith behold its Lord
  Descending in the cloud:
In that revealing Spirit come down,
  Thine attributes proclaim,
And to mine inmost[14] soul make known
  The glories of thy name. (*Ex* 34:5f — *WH* 240)

Imagery? Certainly, but in service of evangelical faith — his faith *beholds*. Or these more celebrated lines:

Ah, shew me that happiest place,
  That place of thy people's abode,
Where saints in an ecstasy gaze,
  And hang on a crucified God:
Thy love for a sinner declare,
  Thy passion and death on the tree;
My spirit to *Calvary* bear,
  To suffer, and triumph, with thee. (*Song of Sol* 1:7 — *HP* 750)

The bold imagery at first shocks us, but then we see it is sublime. 'Happiest' and 'ecstasy' are no selfish luxury of feeling, but are the white heat of devotion to ' a crucified God'. 'Wesley is at the height of his inspiration : nothing short of inspiration keeps the daring emotion sane and reverent and orthodox'.[15] 'Happiest' here is not a term of pure subjectivity but has something of its base-meaning of 'good happening', and the next word confirms this — that happiest *place*. The 'ecstasy' too, deliberate word of a master of words, is almost literally meant, and he is at the place called *Calvary*. This could all be de-poetised (if anyone wished it).

What Wesley is saying thus imaginatively is that the historic cross of Christ is at the heart of Christian experience. Blake's imaginings are far more a philosophy than experience. He is the poet of this philosophy, whereas Wesley is the poet of evangelical experience — a distinction Nicholson missed. He confused experience with imagination, and seemed not to know that evangelical experience is real. Wesley's is the poetry of this experience, and that is why it is quite half untrue to say that he is romantic rather than classical. No more for him than for Wordsworth is there an absolute distinction between the two, or any abandonment to the pure romanticism,[16] or fantasy, of Coleridge, and especially, Blake. For Wesley is *evangelical* — a distinctive category. His hymns are of the evangelical knowledge and experience of God — 'knowledge and vital piety', as he has it in one hymn (*WH* 461), or, as he begins another:

My God! I know, I feel thee mine! (*HP* 740)

NOTES

1. See B.L. Manning, *The Hymns of Wesley and Watts,* pp 83-86.
2. *English Hymns and Hymnwriters,* p 24.
3. 'Dr Watts did not scruple to say that that single poem, "Wrestling Jacob", was worth all the verses he himself had written' — J Wesley's obituary of his brother, Minutes of Conference, 1788.
4. Puritan Conference, 1968 (*The Puritans,* p 203).
5. The nearest Scripture word would perhaps be 'sprinkled' (*Ex* 24:8; *Heb* 10:22; *I Pe* 1:2)
6. Letter to John Wilson, 1800.
7. My italics.
8. TINTERN ABBEY.
9. 'Gentle Jesus' is possibly Wesley's one credible child-piece, though not in vogue today. His later *Hymns for Children* can be quoted to his ridicule. Neither Wesley was an expert in child psychology!
10. Wordsworth's Preface to *Lyrical Ballads.*
11. 'We talk common sense, both in prose and verse, and use no word but in a fixed and determinate sense'. (J Wesley, Preface to 1780 *Collection*).
12. From the euphoric first half of FOR ONE FALLEN FROM GRACE. *MHB* 407 has four of its verses.
13. *II K* 2: 11f; *Ro* 3:24; *Rev* 12:1.
14. As 1780 — hard not to think the original 'utmost' was in error.
15. B.L. Manning, op cit p 29.
16. *Romantic* — 'imaginative, emotional, remote from experience, visionary' (Concise Oxford Dictionary).

3. THE LIVING FAITH

If personal, felt experience in these hymns means doctrine, as we have tried to show, this is equally true the other way round — doctrine means experience, believing from the heart. 'What we have felt' is the whole Christian verity, and this, in turn, is 'the living faith' of experience:

> Inspire the living faith
> Which whosoe'er receives
> The witness in himself he hath
> And consciously believes. (*HP* 325)

So that if it is great doctrine we want of Wesley, then it is to hymns empirical, even mystical, we turn. His purposed hymns of doctrine must sometimes be reckoned among his failures, especially when they come at second-hand and he is versifying somebody else's prose, prosaically, not writing his own poetry from the heart. Most of his *Hymns on the Trinity*[1] are from his head (or another man's!) rather than from his heart. His *Hymns on the Lord's Supper*[2] follow their source less slavishly, so are much better, but are still not his greatest poetry. 'On' is the ominous word for both, suited to his elder contemporary Pope, essayist in verse,[3] but not to Wesley when he fulfils himself as lyrical poet or hymn-writer. His doctrinal hymns that have life are hymns always of experience.

Thus, Wesley's hymns for the Church's Year are of purpose doctrinal, but it is as experimental they succeed. Take his HYMN FOR EASTER-DAY, concerning sheer event that happened, before ever there was Wesley, or we were:

> Love's redeeming work is done,
> Fought the fight, the battle won;
> Lo! our Sun's eclipse is o'er,
> Lo! he sets in blood no more.
>
> Vain the stone, the watch, the seal,
> Christ has burst the gates of hell!
> Death in vain forbids his rise,
> Christ has opened Paradise.

But the end is the eternity of our souls:

> Soar we now where Christ has led,[4]
> Following our exalted Head;
> Made like him, like him we rise,
> Ours the cross — the grave — the skies!

15

> King of glory, soul of bliss,
> Everlasting life is this,
> Thee to know, thy power to prove,
> Thus to sing, and thus to love!

This essentially doctrinal hymn has become a hymn of experience, we might say, in the writing.

But others, not written as seasonal hymns, but directly as experimental, are built on the same doctrinal foundations. Like this great hymn of experience that also begins with the objective fact of Easter:

> Father of Jesus Christ — my Lord,
>   My Saviour and my Head,
> I trust in thee, whose powerful word
> Hath raised him from the dead.

The ensuing verses are all about moral resurrection of the believer:

> In hope, against all human hope,
>   Self-desperate, I believe:
> Thy quickening word shall raise me up,
>   Thou shalt thy Spirit give.

> To thee the glory of thy power
>   And faithfulness I give;
> I shall in Christ, at that glad hour,
>   And Christ in me shall live.   (*WH* 350 — *HP* 693)

The whole is an interpretation of *Romans* 4:16-25, being a hymn of experience secured by essential doctrine. It is all 'if we believe on him that raised up Jesus our Lord from the dead' (v24).

It is in the inwardness of his religion that Wesley is most objectively theological. The more intimate, the more orthodox — that is his amazing ratio. He is the standard hymn-writer of evangelical religion, with its interlocking principal parts of revealed truth and gracious experience. So often, he has not set out to write doctrine as such; but doctrine it is, in the direct language of experience.

> Five bleeding wounds he bears,
>   Received on *Calvary*;
> They pour effectual prayers,
>   They strongly speak for me:
> Forgive him, O forgive, they cry,
> Nor let that ransomed sinner die!

> The Father hears him pray,
>   His dear anointed One;
> He cannot turn away
>   The presence of his Son:
> His Spirit answers to the blood,
> And tells me I am born of God.   (*HP* 217)

Here is the doctrine of the Trinity, the doctrine of the atonement, and touching both the doctrine of the high priesthood of Christ. But it is all Wesley's experience as he writes, and only so did he write it.

Altogether, these hymns, all Wesley's many best, are hymns of doctrine and experience, both. Take this intimately personal verse:

> O for an heart to praise my God,
>   An heart from sin set free,
> An heart that always feels thy blood
>   So freely spilt for me!

It grounds the whole experimental hymn following in the historic atonement by Christ. That is what we often miss from hymns of experience — like the very comparable *O Jesus Christ, grow thou in me*, which tries, so earnestly, to say the same selfless things of devotion to our Lord. We must not scorn a hymn like that, but it is weak in comparison for want of any cardinal doctrine in it — it is *all* experience, and so the experience of *much less*. Again, we would not deride Miss Havergal's Consecration Hymn, or the Christians who sing and mean it; but it has nothing like the strength of:

> God of all power, and truth, and grace,
>   Which shall from age to age endure,
> Whose word, when heaven and earth shall pass,
>   Remains, and stands for ever sure:
>
> That I thy mercy may proclaim,
>   That all mankind thy truth may see,
> Hallow thy great and glorious name,
>   And perfect holiness in me.

For this is grounded in the very doctrine of God, and its consummation is Christ:

> Now let me gain perfection's height,
>   Now let me into nothing fall,
> Be less than nothing in thy sight,
>   And feel

— yes, Wesley's great word of experience, no apology; but now the word incomparably great, the name above every name:

that Christ is all in all.   (*HP* 726)

It is the strength of doctrine in hymns of experience that distinguishes Wesley among hymn-writers.

We may press the point by putting it negatively. It is virtually *only* in terms of experience that Wesley writes greatly about doctrine. Doctrine without experience tends to be, if not weak, then ossified. This from *Hymns on the Trinity* mentioned is only typical of many more there:

> The Lord our God is only One,
>   One is Jehovah the most high;
> Jehovah is his name alone,
>   Who made and fills both earth and sky:
> Jehovah is the Saviour's name,
>   Jehovah is the Spirit's too;
> And Three essentially the same
>   Is the eternal God and true.

It gets worse —

> The name peculiarly divine
>   Which doth his nature best express,
> To the three persons we assign,
>   And each substantial God confess

— before it does get just tolerably better:

> Rivals of his celestial host
>   We triumph here like those above,
> And Father, Son and Holy Ghost
>   The One supreme Jehovah love.   (*Works* vii, p 282)

Oh, Charles! Can this be you? How much of it is even orthodox? Must we not suspect any 'orthodoxy' that would cover in dead words the living God, and pass a quasi-mathematical formula for Father, Son, and Holy Spirit, and try to make grammar say what only poetry and the language of devotion can begin to say? We note the reiterated 'Jehovah', that continues through these hymns. We need not adopt Percy Dearmer's rule that the name be excluded from all Christian hymns,[5] for the God of the Old Testament is the Father of our Lord Jesus Christ, not just the tribal deity of the Hebrews. But we may agree to the point of observing that it is not the name for God that was most often on our Lord's lips and that he taught his followers to use. Its ubiquity is only here in Wesley's hymns. His hymns of experience, which are most of his hymns, usually have the New Testament name:

> With confidence I now draw nigh,
> And Father, Abba, Father, cry!   (*HP* 217)

These 188 *Hymns on the Trinity*, metaphysical exercises, most of them, rather than evangelical hymns, are a singularly barren tract of the generally fertile Wesley country. Only the last 52 are sub-titled *To the Trinity*, and the general tone of these is scarcely different. A certain dignity of worship (as, *Hail, holy, holy, holy Lord*), or this lit by an evangelical earnestness (as, *A thousand oracles Divine — WH 254*), makes occasional compensation for the almost complete loss of lyrical spontaneity and passion. But for real hymns of the Trinity we go elsewhere in Wesley. We have already quoted possibly the greatest of them, *Arise, my soul, arise*; and another fine hymn, *Father, in whom we live*, comes, significantly, from *Hymns for those that seek and those that have Redemption in the Blood of Jesus Christ*. For Wesley, when he follows his truest impulses, and he mostly does, the Trinity is not a formula but a faith, a matter not of mere decent utterance but of living conviction, not a creed (loyal as he is to the historic creeds of the Church), but actually God. See how, quite after the manner of Paul and the New Testament,[6] simply by empirical grasp of the Gospel, he stumbles upon the Christian doctrine of the Godhead and finds himself using, unformulated, the language of Trinitarian devotion:

> Adam descended from above
>   Our loss of Eden to retrieve,
> Great God of universal love,
>   If all the world in thee may live,
> In us a quickening Spirit be,
> And witness, thou hast died for me.[7]

These lines are not smooth-flowing (they almost begin again in the middle), but they are genuine. A mighty scripture[8] has come home to him with all the force of truth. We can follow his mind's working as he freshly grasps it, bit by bit, in bewilderment almost, but with faith and joy. The poetry is rudimentary, but the rudiments are there. The first thing about poetry, and *par excellence* the hymn, is that it is real utterance. It says much for this verse that John kept it.

For final illustration we go back two years to verses of a beautifully simple hymn which show the doctrine taking shape, spontaneously of the Spirit, as in the New Testament. It is Trinitarian, but not formally so with set verses to Father, Son, and Holy Spirit, and then to the whole Trinity. Wesley did write such (I mean the real ones), like *Father, in whom we live* referred to, and that hymn is live with experience. But this is simply to God as we know him experimentally — our Father, now we are reconciled to him in Jesus; the heavenly Adam, living in us; the Holy Ghost, whose temple we are:

> Since the Son hath made me free,
> Let me taste my liberty ---.
>
> Abba, Father! hear thy child,
> Late in Jesus reconciled ---.

Heavenly Adam, Life divine,
Change my nature into thine ---.

Holy Ghost, no more delay;
Come, and in thy temple stay ---.

These verses[9] close the historic *Hymns and Sacred Poems* 1739, part II, which began with the Conversion Hymn. They are pure lyric, the new simple poetry of experience, and they are authentically the religion of the New Testament. They breathe childlikeness more than anything their author ever wrote for children. They are the poetry, the wonder, of Wesley's new birth.

NOTES

1.   1767, based on William Jones of Nayland, *The Catholic Doctrine of the Trinity* (1754; ed 3, 1767).
2.   1745, based on Daniel Brevint, *The Christian Sacrament and Sacrifice* (1673).
3.   AN ESSAY ON CRITICISM, AN ESSAY ON MAN are what they say they are.
4.   Original (*Hymns and Sacred Poems* 1739) read:
     Soar we now, where Christ has led?
     — upsetting the whole balance of the verse, and quite out of keeping with the rest of this fine hymn. *Rep. Verse* reproduces a page of the hymn in Charles's handwriting (facing p 14, from *Richmond Tracts*), and this has the line as we have always known it. The question-mark could have slipped in from the verse preceding.
5.   *Songs of Praise Discussed*, p 267.
6.   *Ro* 8:9-11; *I Co* 12:4-6; *II Co* 13:14; *Eph* 4:4-6; *II Thess* 2:13f; *I Pe* 1:2f; *I Jn* 3:23f; 4:13-15.
7.   *HP* 185, om (*WH* 32:2). The verse was retained in some Methodist hymn books until 1933.
8.   *I Co* 15:45.
9.   Out of original twelve, being *MHB* 568, beautifully matched with the tune CROWLAND.

4. LO! HE COMES

'Come' is the great thrilling word of Advent hymns, and specially Wesley's. It is to begin with the simple indicative of fact — *Christ comes:*

> A Saviour born, in love supreme
> He comes our fallen souls to raise;
> He comes his people to redeem
> With all his plenitude of grace. (*MHB* 141)

But then it is the imperative of glad welcome — *we bid him come:*

> Come, thou long-expected Jesus,
> Born to set thy people free.
>
> . . . . .
>
> Come, Desire of Nations, come,
> Fix in us thy humble home.

All these are of First Advent, Christmas, this last being from perhaps the most celebrated Christmas hymn in our language, *Hark! the herald-angels sing* (as we know it).

But these hymns are more than a nativity tableau, and Wesley's sole fame as a writer of carols rests fortuitously on 'the herald-angels' — actually, not his words. What he is writing about is the 'stupendous height of heavenly love, ... My God incarnated for me'. This is his constant theme, the announcement of God from heaven; and it is significant that Charles Wesley, whose hymns have virtually no natural theology and generally lack the cosmic dimension that we more associate with his brother John and Watts, does use these categories in relation to the Second Person of the Trinity, in terms of the prologue to John's Gospel and *Colossians* 1:

> The invisible appears on earth   (*Col* 1:15)
> The Son of man, the God of heaven. (*MHB* 141)
>
> . . . . .
>
> Hark how all the welkin[1] rings
> 'Glory to the King of Kings!'
>
> Universal nature say
> 'Christ the Lord is born to-day!' (*Rep Verse* 8[2])
>
> . . . . .

21

God comes down, he bows the sky,
  And shews himself our Friend.   (*HP* 101*)*

.   .   .   .   .

When thou in our flesh didst appear,
  All nature acknowledged thy birth.   (*HP* 400)

.   .   .   .

Whom all the angels worship
  Lies hid in human nature;
    Incarnate see
    The Deity,
  The infinite Creator!   (*Rep Verse* 40)

And so in hymn after hymn the poet in Wesley rises to the sublime paradox of
the Word made flesh — not less his serious faith for its imaginative appeal to
him.   He has no intellectual problems with what he cannot explain, and the
poetry is his vehicle for saying, as far as words can ever say, the unutterable:

Our God contracted to a span,
Incomprehensibly made man.

Unmarked by human eye
  The latent Godhead lay.

Suffice for us that God, we know,
Our God is manifest below.   (*HP* 109)

.   .   .   .   .

Being's source *begins* to be,
  And God himself is BORN! (*HP* 101)

.   .   .   .

Veiled in flesh the Godhead see,
Hail the incarnate Deity!

.   .   .   .

O mercy divine,
  How couldst thou incline
My God to become such an infant as *mine*!

Our God ever blest
With oxen doth rest,
Is nursed by his creature and hangs at the breast.

So heavenly mild
His innocence smiled,
No wonder the mother should worship the child!   (*Rep Verse* 5)

John called these last two verses 'namby-pambical'[3], but he need not have
worried, for his brother never wrote the merely pretty carol. Charles never
forgot who this baby is — like mine, but *our God*! That is the orthodox
doctrine of the incarnation, and these verses challenge us to decide whether we
honestly believe it, or not.

Essential, then, to these hymns of First Advent is the Person of him who
comes — his divine identity; and after that, the gospel of his coming. In two
outstanding hymns of Wesley's his coming is as light to a dark world. One we
have already noted:

Stupendous height of heavenly love,
  Of pitying tenderness divine;
It brought the Saviour from above,
  It caused the springing day to shine,
The Sun of Righteousness to appear,
And gild our gloomy hemisphere.

In this opening verse, two scriptures give the picture for the whole hymn —
'the springing day' (*Lk* 1:78), and 'the Sun of Righteousness' (*Mal* 4:2 AV).
His coming is to bring light:

Come then, O Lord, thy light impart.

And it is about light to the hymn's end:

And through the dreary vale unknown
Conduct me to thy dazzling throne.   (*HP* 462)

Almost by accident, this great hymn is overlooked today.[4]

Wesley's other great Advent hymn in the figure of light is also a picture
drawn from Scripture: 'The people that walked in darkness have seen a great
light: they that dwell in the land of the shadow of death, upon them hath the
light shined' (*Isa* 9:2). This hymn not only suffers neglect, but is quite lost
from all our hymnbooks — I can only think through failure to read more than
two lines of it. 'Light of those whose dreary dwelling / Borders on the shades
of death' is maybe not an inviting beginning to a hymn, but what it begins here
is an outstanding hymn of Advent hope, in words and very spirit of Isaiah's
prophecy:

Light of those whose dreary dwelling
    Borders on the shades of death,
Come, and by thy love's revealing
    Dissipate the clouds beneath:
The new heaven and earth's Creator,
    In our deepest darkness rise,
Scattering all the night of nature,
    Pouring eyesight on our eyes.

Still we wait for thy appearing,
    Life and joy thy beams impart,
Chasing all our fears, and cheering
    Every poor benighted heart:
Come, and manifest the favour
    God hath for our ransomed race,
Come, thou universal Saviour,
    Come and bring the gospel grace.

Save us in thy great compassion,
    O thou mild pacific prince;
Give the knowledge of salvation,
    Give the pardon of our sins:
By thine all-restoring merit
    Every burdened soul release;
Every weary, wandering spirit
    Guide into thy perfect peace.   (*MHB* 261)

This is distinctive even among Wesley hymns. I can't recall off-hand another
with so much alliteration, and the letter 'd' looks to be of special interest —
five times in the first two lines, then six in the next four. Some are hidden
mid-word, with quiet effect:

Borders on the shades of death.

These set the tone for the hymn — low-key, but composed. And they come in
again four times in the last three lines, leaving the same final impression —
'burdened', 'wandering', 'guide'. Verse-structure does the same — a subdued
first half of each followed by a second of rising faith and confidence, emphasis
passing from our predicament and need to the gospel-grace of Christ; and at
MHB 261 the tune Saltash (Pleading Saviour), by its lift and sustained high
notes in lines 5 and 6, exactly matched the quickened tempo, to convey the
evangelical difference made when people who walked in darkness now see a
great light.   Then there is significant vocabulary — 'dissipate', 'manifest',
'pacific', none the obvious word, all gospel words in context of the hymn.
And crucially the Advent-word itself, 'Come', by which we address the Lord
at the beginning and which we thrice-repeat in the next verse to greet his
coming. Altogether, these verses convey a true apprehension of who he is

who comes — Creator, Saviour, Prince. In other great hymns Wesley declares even more explicitly that he who comes is God, but this hymn spells out all that that means for the world he comes to.

Another hymn about what Christ's coming means for the world[5] is happily available and known — *All glory to God in the sky*. There is a difference in time-perspective between the two hymns. The one has the note of immediacy and greets the imminent coming, imaginatively as from the dark ages before Christ:

> Come, thou universal Saviour,
>   Come and bring the gospel grace.

This other looks back to his coming, historically:

> Who meanly in Bethlehem born
>   Didst stoop to redeem a lost race.

So the bidding 'Come' in this hymn means his coming again:

> Once more to thy creatures return,
>   And reign in thy kingdom of grace.

> Come then to thy servants again,
>   Who long thy appearing to know.   (*HP* 400)

But this future coming is 'not in an Apocalypse but through the indwelling power of Christ in the hearts of men and women'.[6] This meets the modern mood and is clearly in advance of its time (neither better nor worse for that — it is how truth fares that matters). Wesley's great longing, and ours today, is for peace on earth, and he follows Milton in the pious legend that there actually was peace on the night of Christ's coming:

> When thou in our flesh didst appear,
>   All nature acknowledged thy birth;
> Arose the acceptable year
>   And heaven was opened on earth.

This echoes the Nativity Ode:

> No War, or battail's sound ---.

> But peaceful was the night ---.

The verse ends with words from the collect for peace, about

> The giver of concord and love,
>   The prince and the author of peace.

This is a fine hymn, though it does not have the sense of immediate or imminent coming that characterises Wesley at his very greatest. Here, he longs for Christ's coming rather than announces it:

> O wouldst thou again be made known,
>   Again in thy Spirit descend.

John Wesley judged this best of his brother's *Hymns for the Nativity of our Lord*[3] — and if they had been anybody else's hymns, that would surely have been so.

A supreme Wesley hymn of Advent is not recognised for what it is:[7]

> Love divine, all loves excelling,
>   Joy of heaven to earth come down ...
> Visit us with thy salvation,
>   Enter every trembling heart.
>
> Come, almighty to deliver,
>   Let us all thy life receive;
> Suddenly return, and never,
>   Never more thy temples leave.

This is undubitably Advent, but it is a hymn on its own and difficult to classify. Is it a hymn of the Second Advent? It is, but not as simply and directly as 'Lo! he comes'. 'Suddenly return' is certainly the language of apocalypse (*Mal* 3:1; *Mk* 13:36; *I.Thess* 5:2f), and he who shall so return is 'Jesus all compassion' to whom the whole hymn is addressed. It was not, of course, written as a theological statement, but is a characteristic Wesley hymn of experience, and not untheological for that. Its overall theme is the ultimacy of Christian experience, with perhaps a hint of the rapture of the saints, and then heaven (*IICo.* 3:18; *Rev* 4:10):

> Changed from glory into glory,
>   Till in heaven we take our place,
> Till we cast our crowns before thee,
>   Lost in wonder, love and praise.

There remain Wesley's hymns proper of Second, that is Final, Advent, for which he did not hesitate to use all the New Testament imagery. There will be an end to this world-order, when the tangent of history touches the circle of eternity in unprecendented and indescribable event. That event, history and yet no longer history, we can only begin to describe in pictures — how literally, for instance, are we to understand meeting the Lord in the air? (*I.Thess* 4:17). But it is real event in terms of Jesus Christ, his advent, the final revelation of him (*I.Pe* 1:7). 'Lo! he comes' will assuredly happen. It will mark the consummation, in time and for eternity, of the kingdom of God. (*I.Co* 15:24f):

> Saviour, take the power and glory,
> Claim the kingdom for thine own.   (*HP* 241)

Wesley's other hymns of Final Advent, and of course anybody else's, must rank after that. But some ought to be better known than they are. *Ye virgin souls arise (WH* 64) might have been but for its beginning — some may have difficulty in thinking of themselves as 'virgin souls' (such is literalism![8]). But what we are missing is a superb dramatic presentation, and application to ourselves, of our Lord's parable of the Virgins (*Mt* 25: 1-13). Doddridge's unexciting rendering of a related parable, *Ye servants of the Lord (Lk* 12:35-38), has gained far more acceptance in hymnbooks, but one wonders why. It has nothing to match:

> Upstarting at the midnight cry,
> Behold the heavenly bridegroom nigh!
>
> Made ready for your full reward,
> Go forth with joy to meet your Lord!
>
> Far from a world of grief, and sin,
> With God eternally shut in!

The tenor of this whole hymn is preparedness, and two more Wesley hymns of Advent watch invite comparison. *Hearken to the solemn voice WH* 53), on the same parable, is an evangelical hymn that combines doctrine and experience in a way that is nearly uniquely Wesley's own:

> Go ye forth to meet your Lord,
> And meet him in your heart.

Thou Judge of quick and dead, most sombre of the three, has surprisingly survived into *Hymns and Psalms*, perhaps for one magnificent verse:

> To pray, and wait the hour,
> The awful hour unknown,
> When robed in majesty, and power,
> Thou shalt from heaven come down,
> The immortal Son of Man,
> To judge the human race,
> With all thy Father's dazzling train,
> With all thy glorious grace.   (*HP* 247)

All three hymns are admonitory (not best for hymns, required for these hymns), but the other two have more the note of glad anticipation and welcome of the Lord.

We may add here two fine New Year hymns which are essentially Advent, for Wesley never thinks of time but as leading to end-time and eternity — 'the millennial year', 'the day of his coming', 'the jubilee of heaven':

> The arrow is flown,
> The moment is gone,
> The millennial year
> Rushes on to our view, and eternity's here.
>
> O that each in the day
> Of his coming might say,
> 'I have fought my way through,
> I have finished the work thou didst give me to do!' (*HP* 354)

Even Methodists may consider themselves fortunate they still have that, for they lost the magnificent ending of *Sing to the great Jehovah's praise* as long ago as 1933:

> Till Jesus in the clouds appear
>   To saints on earth forgiven,
> And bring the grand sabbatic year,
>   The jubilee of heaven. (*Rep Verse* 89)

But can we sing such hymns today? I ask another question — why should such imagery be acceptable in *Lo! he comes,* admittedly greatest of them all, and not in other fine Advent hymns?

Advent is about him who came and shall come — not ambiguously, as though we might intend either meaning by an Advent hymn. Rather, that First Advent holds the promise of Final Advent, so that he who came in great humility shall come again in his glorious majesty. Each Advent we enter imaginatively into the hope of his coming, and in these hymns it is proleptically now — 'realised eschatology', we might almost say, *in the sense* of experience:

> Lo! he comes with clouds descending.

This Wesley hymn is still mixed up in hymnbooks with its inferiors, Cennick's original and Madan's cento of the two, but his is incomparable in its vividness, its presentness, that cuts through all remaining time and brings us *there:*

> Every eye shall now behold him

— no two Wesley words together are more characteristic than 'shall now'; and:

> With what rapture
> Gaze we on those glorious scars!

28

Christ ascended is still God incarnate with scars to show. His incarnation and passion were historical, and are eternal. I used to wonder why we celebrate Final Advent along with First Advent, with some possible confusion. Ought it not to follow Ascension and Pentecost? There would be reason in that. But the Church's instinct was profounder. It is the same divine Person who comes, and that is Advent. He comes at end-time who came at the fulness of time and was once for favoured sinners slain. It is the Saviour who takes the power and glory and claims the kingdom for his own:

> Yea, amen! let all adore thee,
>   High on thine eternal throne;
> Saviour, take the power and glory,
>   Claim the kingdom for thine own:
>   JAH, JEHOVAH,
>   Everlasting God, come down!

NOTES

1.   'Welkin' — sky, or upper air.
2.   Of course original of the long-unassailable *Hark! the herald-angels sing.*
3.   In a letter to Charles, 26 12 61 (*Works* iv, p xii).
4.   That is because the two current hymnbooks which have it do not present it as Advent. *HP* puts it in a section *People of the Light*, attractively, but at the too high cost of losing it from the Church's Year. Even its Liturgical Index does not direct us to it for its proper season, Advent and then Epiphany. *Christian Hymns* also has the credit of this hymn, but likewise hidden away — 737.
5.   Yet another, *My heart is full of Christ,* I leave out only because, following Bett, I make it John's.
6.   *Companion to HP,* p 248.
7.   Classified 'General', or under some general head, in hymnbooks without exception, and is even used as a wedding hymn — I take it for the mere opening word 'love', and also perhaps as excuse for a too-popular tune that bids to smother the words. Anyway, the true meaning of the hymn, and its proper use, are quite lost.
8.   *Christian Hymns,* which has the merit of restoring the hymn, slightly tailored to Calvinist requirements, has 'slumbering souls' (296).

5. WITH WESLEY THROUGH
THE CHURCH'S YEAR

That Charles Wesley is the standard hymnwriter of Christian experience few will question who speak English with any sensitivity and have any conception what it is to experience Christ. That he is standard for hymns of the Church seasons is less widely recognised. But it is Wesley who has provided, in virtually unbroken series, a unique corpus of hymns of the Christian revelation of God, set down in Scripture and celebrated by the Church in her ordered worship-progression of Advent to Trinity. This liturgical use is a not indispensable but immensely useful frame of doctrinal worship, within which Wesley's whole edifice is theological and strong. As Manning said once for all, 'Nothing is more untrue than to represent the heart of Wesley's religion as personal experience or even personal feeling. The heart of Wesley's religion is sound doctrine.'[1] How odd then that hymnbook compilers who attach importance to the Church's Year (commendably) should so regularly under-assess Wesley's supreme importance for this!

Advent we have treated separately, to include Christmas, and Epiphany is only an aspect of these. Wesley has no hymn directly on the story of the Magi. His nearest might be two verses of a hymn, or carol, mainly on the Shepherd story, and they certainly merit notice:

> The wise men adore,
> And bring him their store;
> The rich are permitted to follow the poor.

> To the inn they repair
> To see the young heir;
> The inn is a palace, for Jesus is there! (*Rep Verse* 50[2])

But he has nothing like, say, *As with gladness*. His one labelled HYMN FOR THE EPIPHANY[3] is more on the doctrinal theme of 'a light to the nations; (*Is* 42:6), but for this, *Light of those whose dreary dwelling, Head of thy Church, whose Spirit fills,* and, more personalised, *Stupendous height of heavenly love* are better to be remembered. These are Advent hymns overall:

> Come, thou universal Saviour.

> Answer the universal 'Come!'

> Come then, O Lord, thy light impart.

Advent is the comprehensive and theological word, with its cardinal doctrine of him who comes,

The Son of man, the God of heaven. (*MHB* 141)

It is on this basis of the Person of our Lord that Wesley, in keeping with orthodox Christianity, builds in his hymns the other cardinal doctrines of the Faith — passion, resurrection, ascension, and the coming of the Spirit.

Lenten hymns we may pass over here, for whilst Wesley has many fine devotional and penitential hymns suitable for Lent as we generally observe it, these are not specifically about first Lent, Christ's Lent, with his baptism, temptations and dedication to the cross.[5]

So the next main group of Wesley seasonal hymns is those for the Passion. They are of the same stuff as his Advent hymns, being about a Person — not a philosophy of incarnation, but God incarnate; not abstractly a cross, but Christ crucified. For the difference, take:

> When the woes of life o'ertake me,
> Hopes deceive and fears annoy,
> Never shall the Cross forsake me,
> Lo! it glows with peace and joy

— and the rest. Is this really what the hymn began by announcing, the cross of Christ in which I glory? Where is Christ? Wesley has no doubt where:

> See him stretched on yonder cross   (*HP* 166)

— that cross, unique and saving. Or consider:

> O Cross that liftest up my head,
> I dare not ask to fly from thee:
> I lay in dust life's glory dead,
> And from the ground there blossoms red
> Life that shall endless be.

These most celebrated lines of their author are to our purpose because so comparable with Wesley in imagination and emotion, and indeed sincerity, yet so lacking the character of a Wesley hymn. There is nothing scriptural here, and specifically not the cross of Gospel record. We cannot but regard with dubiety this hypostatizing the cross — there is no Saviour on this cross. And then no risen Lord, for all the moving words about resurrection. We sense more of Proserpine and the year's renewal than of Jesus and the resurrection. But everywhere in Wesley's Passion hymns is devotion to a Person:

> For ever here my rest shall be,
> Close to thy bleeding side;
> This all my hope, and all my plea,
> For me the Saviour died!   (*MHB* 456)

.   .   .   .   .

31

Come then, and to my soul reveal
   The heights and depths of grace,
Those wounds which all my sorrows heal,
   That dear disfigured face. (*HP* 184)

    .   .   .   .

O let me kiss thy bleeding feet,
   And bathe, and wash them with my tears. (*HP* 185)

    .   .   .   .

By thine agonising pain
   And bloody sweat, we pray,
By thy dying love to man
   Take all our sins away ...
O remember *Calvary*,
   And bid us go in peace. (*HP* 550)

    .   .   .   .

See, Lord, the travail of thy soul
   Accomplished in the change of mine;
And plunge me, every whit made whole,
   In all the depths of love divine! (*WH* 396)

Wesley's fundamental paradox of the cross is 'immortal God' who dies:

O Love divine, what hast thou done!
   The immortal God hath died for me!
The Father's co-eternal Son
   Bore all my sins upon the tree:
The immortal God for me hath died!
My Lord, my Love is crucified! (*HP* 175)

    .   .   .   .

With glorious clouds encompassed round,
   Whom angels dimly see,
Will the unsearchable be found,
   Or God appear to me?

In manifested love explain
   Thy wonderful design;
What meant the suffering Son of Man,
   The streaming blood divine?

> I view the Lamb in his own light
> > Whom angels dimly see,
> And gaze transported at the sight
> > Through all eternity. (*HP* 184)

This is again the cosmic dimension we noted in the Advent hymns, and Wesley's supreme poetry of it is more than we can sing:

> Jesus drinks the bitter cup,
> > The wine-press treads alone,
> Tears the graves and mountains up
> > By his expiring groan:
> Lo! the powers of hell he shakes,
> > Nature in convulsions lies,
> Earth's profoundest centre quakes,
> > The great Jehovah dies!
>
> Dies the glorious cause of all,
> > The true eternal Pan,
> Falls to raise us from our fall,
> > To ransom sinful man:
> Well may Sol withdraw his light,
> > With the sufferer sympathize,
> Leave the world in sudden night
> > While his Creator dies.
>
> Well may heaven be clothed in black
> > And solemn sackcloth wear,
> Jesu's agony partake,
> > The hours of darkness share:
> Mourn the astonied hosts above,
> > Silence saddens all the skies;
> Kindler of seraphic love,
> > The God of angels dies! (*Rep Verse* 54)[6]

Here is nature, but not for its own sake or with any concern for natural theology. It is nature in light of revelation, and witnessing to revealed truth. The bold classical allusions, using the very language of paganism for the doctrine of God the Creator, pass quite beyond the use of hymns, but the cumulative force of:

> The great Jehovah dies!

> While his Creator dies!

> The God of angels dies!

makes this one of the most solemn and moving poems about the cross anywhere.

But this is not patripassionism, or some ridiculous death-of-God 'theology'. It is the orthodox doctrine of God, and Wesley never fails, least of all in contemplation of the cross, to make the distinction between the Father and the Son:

> 'Forgive them, Father, O forgive!
> They know not that by me they live' (*HP* 185)

> .　.　.　.　.

> Who made intercession, 'My Father, forgive!'

And because God is the Father of Jesus, I too can call him Father:

> O Father, thou know'st he hath died in my place! (*MHB* 188)

The atonement lies precisely in the relation of the Father to the incarnate Son. These hymns have the balance and profundity of New Testament doctrine, by which both 'God was in Christ reconciling' and 'He made him to be sin for us' (*II Co* 5:19,21):

> See him stretched on yonder cross,
> And crushed beneath our load.

> Faith cries out, 'Tis he, 'tis he,
> My God, that suffers there! (*HP* 166)

Wesley's hymns for Easter and Ascension follow on from his Advent and Passion hymns in asserting the unique deity of Christ; and particularly they acclaim him in his heavenly place and station. In them, Easter and Ascension are scarcely to be distinguished from each other. The Methodist practice of putting both together in one hymnbook section may reflect this. Alphabetical arrangement in the latest edition has the effect now of jumbling the hymns rather oddly, but Wesley's among them may be some precedent for the single grouping. Thus, having sung

> Christ the Lord is risen today

we go on to sing, still on Easter morning.

> Soar we now where Christ has led,
> Following our exalted Head.

Similar is his exposition of *Colossians* 3:1-4, which makes the transition in one double-verse (as he wrote it) from

If risen with him indeed ye are ...
His resurrection's power declare

to

And seek the glorious things above,
And follow Christ your Head to heaven.   (*HP* 751)

And it is interesting to note that *Rejoice, the Lord is King!* was first published in *Hymns for our Lord's Resurrection*, though it is clearly an Ascension hymn:

Jesus the Saviour reigns,
The God of truth and love;
When he had purged our stains,
He took his seat above.

We cannot separate these hymns.
And it is the heavenliness of Christ they are all about:

He took his seat above.

. . . . .

Christ, awhile to mortals given,
Re-ascends his native heaven.

This means one supreme thing about him, who he is:

God is gone up on high   (*MHB* 219)

. . . . .

The God of truth and love.

. . . . .

God over all, for ever blest!   (*HP* 206)

And as with the Advent and Passion hymns, whilst Wesley does not hesitate to call Christ God, this is on the precise Trinitarian definition of the Godhead. Christ is the eternal Son of God, who intercedes with the Father for us:

He pleads his passion on the tree,
He shows himself to God for me.

35

> My name is graven on his hands,
>   And him the Father always hears. (*MHB* 232)

. . . . .

> The Father hears him pray,
>   His dear anointed one;
> He cannot turn away
>   The presence of his Son. (*HP* 217)

In all, these hymns of Advent to Ascension present the full doctrine of Christ from the New Testament, only to be complemented by hymns of the Holy Spirit's witness to Christ.

The first thing to be said about these hymns of the Spirit (and uncounted references in not-expressly Whitsun hymns) is that they are hymns about God — a truism, but with Wesley true at depth. 'His witness is within', in Whittier's phrase, but it is *the Holy Spirit* who witnesses with our spirit (*Ro* 8:16). He is not our spirit, and not other, in very immanence, than transcendent God:

> God, the everlasting God,
> Makes with mortals his abode;
> Whom the heavens cannot contain,
> He vouchsafes to dwell in man.

> ... the gift and Giver too. (*HP* 287)

This is the evangelical paradox, indeed, which captures Wesley's poetic imagination (and so it ought), but which is his serious and profound theology. It is never *mere* immanentism, there is always the heavenly dimension. Wesley is not interested in

> The sunshine ... of God
> The life of man and flower,
> The wisdom and the energy
>   That fills the world with power (*MHB* 279)

(whatever of truth may be in Dearmer's lines), but in

> The witness of Jesus returned to his home. (*HP* 296)

And it would take no form-critic to tell which of these is his — this:

> Thought answereth alone to thought,
>   And soul with soul hath kin;
> The outward God he findeth not
>   Who finds not God within (*MHB* 281)

or this:

> The pledge of our Lord
> To his heaven restored
> Is sent from the sky,
> And tells us our Head is exalted on high.   (*HP* 296)

Wesley's understanding is the exact opposite of Hosmer's — we do not find the inward God except he be Christ-sent from above.

Faith that is by the Holy Spirit is *the faith* of the Church, and only by him can we seriously repeat the Church's most fundamental creed:

> No man can truly say
> That Jesus is the Lord,
> Unless thou take the veil away
> And breathe the living word:
> Then, only then we feel
> Our interest in his blood,
> And cry, with joy unspeakable,
> Thou art my Lord, my God!   (*I Co* 15:3; *HP* 325)

These are surely Wesley's most distinguished hymns of all, distinguished from most other hymns of the Spirit for being directly about Christ and Christ's own promise, 'He shall glorify me, for he shall receive of mine, and shall shew it unto you' (*Jn* 16:14). The Holy Spirit is teacher:

> That heavenly teacher of mankind,
> That guide infallible impart,
> To bring thy sayings to our mind
> And write them on our faithful heart.   (*MHB* 275)

He is preacher:

> True recorder of his passion,
> Now the living faith impart,
> Now reveal his great salvation,
> Preach his gospel to our heart.
>
> Come, thou witness of his dying,
> Come, remembrancer divine;
> Let us feel thy power, applying
> Christ to every soul and mine.   (*HP* 298)

He is evangelist:

37

Spirit of faith, within us live,
    And strike the crowd with fixed amaze;
Open our mouths, and utterance give
    To publish our Redeemer's praise:

To testify the grace of God,
    Today as yesterday the same,
And spread throughout the earth abroad
    The wonders wrought by Jesu's name.[7]

And it was even so — the Evangelical Revival, out of which Wesley wrote. Beginning with first Pentecost, the coming of the Spirit has always meant the new powerful witness to Christ. How many other hymns quite say this?

I have always felt that the Church's Year of Advent to Trinity is more than a liturgical arrangement. It is the right theological order, for the Christian knowledge of God begins with Christ. The whole plan of worship is Trinitarian — God in Christ through the Spirit. Trinity Sunday is then the issue of all that has led up to it — the sum of revelation. This order reflects the first Christianity, which came to the truth of God evangelically. And Wesley does, too. His formal hymns of the Trinity are not generally his best, or most characteristic. It is his hymns of Advent to Pentecost, with their grasp of our Lord's deity and the Holy Spirit's witness to him, Trinitarian all along, that are the heart of his doctrine. His most impressive hymns of the Trinity are where he has not set out to write any such thing — witness this for unconscious orthodoxy (we have already quoted it):

The Father hears him pray,
    His dear anointed one;
He cannot turn away
    The presence of his Son:
His Spirit answers to the blood,
And tells me I am born of God.   (*HP* 217)

Such, then, are Wesley's hymns for the Church's Year, and they form a complete liturgy of her Trinitarian faith. 'We have almost nothing to learn even liturgically that we cannot learn from Wesley'[8] was Manning's justified conclusion. In providing so impressive a liturgy,[9] Wesley has produced, largely unknowing, a systematic theology that can stand alongside any the Church has known, 'the full-orbed and conscious orthodoxy of a scholar trained and humbled as he contemplates the holy, catholic and evangelical faith in its historic glory and strength'.[10]

And yet, though experience is no substitute for doctrine, these great doctrinal hymns of Advent to Trinity *are* all hymns of experience. That is the wonder of them, and where Wesley excels even the great John Mason Neale, who has given us so many of the historic hymns of the Church's faith. Perhaps no other hymnwriter than Wesley has even attempted to write *experimentally* for the Church's Year. And we would not quite say that

Wesley made the attempt — he spontaneously did it. His experience is authentic because his doctrine is true. From

> Answer thy mercy's whole design,
>   My God incarnated for me,   (*HP* 462)

through

> O remember Calvary,
>   And bid us go in peace! (*HP* 550)

and

> Made like him,[11] like him we rise,
> Ours the cross — the grave — the skies! (*HP* 193)

to

> The length and breadth of love reveal,
>   The height and depth of Deity;
> And all the sons of glory seal,
>   And change, and make us all like thee![12]

these are all hymns of experience. Wesley is unique among hymnwriters not for doctrine (though how sure the doctrine is!), or experience (how authentic that is!), but for their unity and identity in his hymns.

————————————

NOTES

1. B.L. Manning, *The Hymns of Wesley and Watts*, p 75.
2. *O mercy divine*, quoted in our previous paper.
3. *Sons of men, behold from far* (*Works*, i p 184). It is the only one of an early group of Church seasonal hymns in the same 4 7s metre that has not achieved merited fame. The others: *HP* 106, 193, 197, 287. They are all hymns of celebration, which may explain the absence of one for Passiontide.
4. *HP* has this among the Pentecost hymns (316), on strength of the first two verses. But it is clearly an Advent and Epiphany hymn.
5. Anglican hymnbooks have picked out for Lent *O for a heart to praise my God*, and this can be supplemented by many more Wesley holiness hymns. The theme of temptation, as *HP* 720, *MHB* 476, is closer to Lent, but even these are scarcely to be counted in the theological corpus of Wesley's seasonal hymns.
6. Further verses of *HP* 166.
7. Further and final verses of *HP* 307.
8. Manning, op cit, p 42.

9.   Cranmer and Charles Wesley are the two great names in English liturgy, and one could wish that Anglicans and Methodists better knew this today.
10. Manning, op cit, p 27.
11. That is, made to be, by grace — *Ro* 8:29; *2 Pe* 1:4; *1 Jn* 3:2; 4-17.
12. End of Pentecost hymn quoted, *MHB* 275.

6. IN ALL THE SCRIPTURES

No Bible expositor can have been in principle more Christian than Charles Wesley, for he found Christ in all the Scriptures — of course with Christ's authority for doing so (*Lk* 24:27, 44-47; *Jn* 5:39):

> Sole Subject of the sacred book,
> Thou fillest all, and thou alone.   (*Works* iv, p. 136)

Now that is not literally true — the Bible is about Abraham and Ahab and all sorts of people, and Methodists felt embarrassed enough to alter it to 'Chief subject', till in 1933 they dropped the hymn.   But what Wesley was profoundly saying *is* true — a whole evangelic history of which the finality and comprehensive meaning is Christ. 'Whole subject' might be better when the hymn is restored.   Wesley's hymns, almost totally, are about Christ in all the Scriptures.

Wesley was not the pioneer of this, but Watts was.   His *Hymns and Spiritual Songs,* 1707 (Wesley's birth year), has a first section of 150 *Collected from the Holy Scriptures.*   A lively preface anticipates criticism from 'those who think nothing must be sung unto God but the Translations of his own Word'.   Against this he announces paraphrase with 'the Levitical Ceremonies and Hebrew forms of speech changed into the Worship of the Gospel', and still more radically projects a Psalter which has 'David converted into a Christian'.   That came twelve years later, a bold challenge to the older use and orthodoxy — *The Psalms of David Imitated in the Language of the New Testament and applied to the Christian State and Worship.* This Christianizing is not explicit in many of these psalms, but some outstanding ones *are* explicitly Christian.   The messianic *Ps* 72 becomes *Jesus shall reign.* In Ps 122, 'the thrones of the house of David' are the royal throne of David's greater Son — and grace is added to judgement, indeed comes first:

> There David's greater Son
> Has fixed his royal throne;
> He sits for grace and judgement there.

John 1:17 is introduced into *Ps* 103 with such symmetry that it is hard to think it was not always there:

> His wondrous works and ways
> He made by Moses known,
> But sent the world his truth and grace
> By his beloved Son.

What Watts did was to claim the Old Testament for the Gospel of the New — which, though it shocked the orthodox, was a very orthodox thing to do.   'The evangeliser of the Psalter', as Josiah Conder called him, fought the main battle over this, and the measure of his success was the ease and naturalness with which Wesley, only his younger contemporary, could assume it and in propitious circumstances of the Evangelical Revival carry it much further. Wesley's freedom of his Bible is taken for granted in his hymns, but this was in God's providence Watts's legacy to him. As long as we are clear that the best of the older psalmody, headed by Kethe's incomparable hundredth, has not been superseded, we can only welcome the newness of the New Testament as Watts, and even more Wesley, bring it to bear upon the interpretation of the Old.

Wesley went in and possessed the land won for him. He too, and more completely, produced the evangelised psalm — not bare paraphrase but Christian hymn. Compare his 23rd psalm with the admirable versions we all know. Watts had exercised freedom in rendering the psalm, and its last verse is so delightful, I cannot resist digressing to quote it:

> There would I find a settled rest
> While others go and come,
> No more a stranger or a guest
> But like a child at home.

But the whole is still in compass of the Old Testament:

> My Shepherd will supply my need,
> Jehovah is his name.

Herbert and Watts, allusively, and H. W. Baker directly, bring the parable of the Lost Sheep into the psalm — I need not quote. But Wesley's version is a whole interpretation in terms of John 10, and he has the highest authority for this. For our Lord, in declaring himself the good shepherd, is surely claiming the shepherd psalm as his own, so that ' the Lord my shepherd' in the psalm is he in the gospel who now lays down his life for the sheep:

> He in sickness makes me whole,
>   Guides into the paths of peace;
> He revives my fainting soul,
>   Stablishes in righteousness:
> Who for me vouchsafed to die,
> Loves me still — I know not why. (*HP* 263)

Wesley has many such, like his Ascension psalm (24 ii), which also identifies the Lord with Jesus:

> Who is the King of glory, who?
>   The Lord that all his foes o'ercame,
> The world, sin, death and hell o'erthrew:
>   And Jesus is the conqueror's name. (*HP* 206)

Again, Wesley's *Ps* 48:

> Sion's God is all our own,
>   Who on his love rely;
> We his pardoning love have known,
>   And live to Christ, and die. (*HP* 438)

Or his 121st — no substitute for the plain beauty of the Scottish version, but its proper evangelical supplement:

> Christ shall bless thy going out,
>   Shall bless thy coming in,
> Kindly compass thee about
>   Till thou art saved from sin:
> Like thy spotless Master thou,
>   Filled with wisdom, love, and power,
> Holy, pure, and perfect now,
>   Henceforth and evermore. (*MHB* 497)

But Wesley's New Testament interpretations of the Old range far beyond the Psalms, over virtually the whole Testament. Often he touches the borderline of paraphrase — recognisable, but free, and importantly, Christian. Supreme among them is WRESTLING JACOB — out of Israel's remote past, Wesley's present Christian experience:

> Art thou the Man that died for me?
>   The secret of thy love unfold.
>
> And when my all of strength shall fail,
>   I shall with the God-man prevail

— it is Christ he wrestles with, and in consequence he is granted what was not granted to Moses (*Ex* 33: 18-23):

> Through faith I see thee face to face,
>   I see thee face to face, and live.

In his own way, Wesley has come through to Watts's great New Testament affirmation already quoted — it will bear repetition:

> His wondrous works and ways
>   He made by Moses known,
> But sent the world his truth and grace
>   By his beloved Son.

But Wesley goes incredibly further, and right through his Old Testament reads Christ:

Now, O my Joshua, bring me in!
Cast out my foes; the inbred sin,
   The carnal mind remove;
The purchase of thy death divide,
And O! with all the sanctified
   Give me a lot of love.   (WH 392 — Num 27: 15-18; Josh 14:2)

. . . . .

Jesu, attend, thyself reveal!
   Are we not met in thy great name?
Thee in the midst we wait to feel,
   We wait to catch the spreading flame.   (MHB 710; I K 18:37f)

(Likewise HP 740: 5-7, in prayer to Jesus with invocation of the Holy Spirit).

. . . . .

Though the sons of night blaspheme,
More there are with us than them;
God with us, we cannot fear;
Fear, ye fiends, for Christ is here!   (HP 811; IIK 6:16)

. . . . .

Riches of Christ on all bestowed...

Wisdom, and Christ, and heaven are one.   (HP 674; Prov 3:13-19)

. . . . .

   Come, all whoe'er have set
      Your faces Sion-ward,
   In Jesus let us meet
      And praise our common Lord:
In Jesus let us still walk on,
Till all appear before his throne.   (MHB 606)

. . . . .

   Come, let us use the grace divine,
      And all, with one accord,
   In a perpetual covenant join
      Ourselves to Christ the Lord.   (HP 649; Jer 50:5)

(Fascinatingly, Wesley uses different parts of the same Scripture text in quite different hymns.)

.   .   .   .   .

> Give me a new, a perfect heart,
>   From doubt, and fear, and sorrow free;
> The mind which was in Christ impart,
>   And let my spirit cleave to thee.
>
> Cause me to walk in Christ my way,
>   And I thy statutes shall fulfil,
> In every point thy law obey,
>   And perfectly perform thy will. (*Ezek* 36:26f)

Wesley has many verses like these, as well as whole hymns based on an Old Testament text or passage and declaring Christ.   Such is, *O great mountain, who art thou?*, on *Zechariah* 4:6f:

> Not by human might or power,
>   Canst thou be moved from hence,
> But thou shalt bow down before
>   Divine omnipotence:
> My Zerubbabel is near,
>   I have not believed in vain;
> Thou, when Jesus doth appear,
>   Shalt sink into a plain.   (*WH* 371)

Perhaps that is less a hymn to be sung than a poem to be remembered, but hymns to sing include:

O thou who camest from above.	(*Lev* 6.13)
Jesus, let all thy lovers shine.	(*Judg* 5:31)
Thou Shepherd of Israel, and mine.	(*Song of Sol* 1:7)
To the haven of thy breast.	(*Is* 32:2)
Thee, Jesus, full of truth and grace.	(*Dan* 3:24f)

These are all prayers to our Lord.

One more of these hymns to Christ might be our key to all the others — *Oft I in my heart have said*. Its immediate source is the New Testament (*Ro* 10:6-10), but the New had taken it from the Old (*Dt* 30: 11-14), interpreting this as Christian scripture.   In the other examples, direct from the Old Testament, Wesley has done the same.   In reading Christ, he sees through New Testament eyes:

But the righteousness of faith
  Hath taught me better things;
Inward turn thine eyes, it saith,
  While Christ to me it brings;
Christ is ready to impart
  Life to all for life who sigh;
In thy mouth and in thy heart
  The word is ever nigh.   (*HP* 530)

But Wesley goes further than reading Christ in the Old Testament spiritually. He follows the traditional reading of certain scriptures as prophetic of the historical life, death and resurrection of Jesus:

Late in time behold him come,
Offspring of a virgin's womb.

Pleased as man with men to appear
Jesus, our Immanuel here! (*Is* 7:14 AV)

Hail the heavenly Prince of Peace! (*Is* 9:6)
Hail the Sun of Righteousness!
Light and life to all he brings,
Risen with healing in his wings. (*Mal* 4:2 AV)

Come, Desire of Nations, come,
Fix in us thy humble home;   (*Hagg* 2:7 AV)
Rise, the woman's conquering seed,
Bruise in us the serpent's head. (*Rep Verse* 8 — *HP* 106; *Gen* 3:15)

. . . . .

Those wounds which all my sorrows heal, (*Is* 53:5)
  That dear disfigured face.   (*HP* 184; *Is* 52:14)

. . . . .

See, Lord, the travail of thy soul
  Accomplished in the change of mine. (*WH* 396; *Is* 53:11)

. . . . .

Ye that pass by, behold the Man. (*WH* 24; *Lam* 1:12)
(Also *MHB* 186:2; 188:1)

. . . . .

I know that my Redeemer lives,
  And ever prays for me.   (*HP* 731; *Job* 19:25 AV)

And finally his coming again:

> Suddenly return, and never,
> Never more thy temples leave. (*Mal* 3:1)

But how far can we follow Wesley in all this? The references to the King James Version, besides delighting us, should give us pause, for they do indicate possible other readings, with scholarly support, and these may not as certainly mean Christ. A linked consideration is the whole tenor of a passage, which again may not readily confirm the older interpretation of a particular text in it. Thus *Isaiah* 7:14, where 'young woman' rather than 'virgin' is certainly possible, and the context would support this. Granted that 'virgin' here has not got to be wrong, and any way that the doctrine of the Virgin Birth does not depend on its being right, the whole passage (v 10-16) seems to be about a merely human messiah, another Davidic King in the then foreseeable future. And we might come to like conclusions about other Wesley key texts that depend on the Authorised Version. For only one more example, is Job's 'vindicator' (19:25 RV mg) precisely Redeemer as we should understand the title from the New Testament? In fine, *is* Christ in all the Scriptures? We must consider well here, or we might find ourselves querying our Lord's own claims, attested by two evangelic witnesses (as we noted at the beginning). It is precisely here that Wesley can help us.

Take his great hymn JESHURUN — can we honestly find Christ in the passage paraphrased (*Deut* 33: 26-29)? He is certainly not named there, under any title. But Wesley, in saying 'yes', is in line with the whole tenor of the New Testament. This passage, with the Old Testament generally, is about *Israel*. But Israel was born of promise — a special providential history of God's people that should reach beyond itself into all history and to all peoples (*Gen* 12: 2f; 15:5 17: 4-8; 22:17f; 28:13-15). This promise first made to Abraham is taken up by the New Testament and referred to Christ (*Ac* 3: 25f; *Ro* 4: 16-25; *Gal* 3: 14-29). Now all this, about Abraham's faith, 'was not written for his sake alone... but for us also... if we believe on him that raised up Jesus our Lord from the dead' (Ro *4: 23f*). The issue and outcome of the promise, and so the total meaning of the history, is Christ: 'If ye be Christ's, then ye are Abraham's seed, and heirs according to the promise' (*Gal* 3:29). So, whilst these actual words from *Deuteronomy* are not in the New Testament, it is entirely in the spirit of the New Testament that Wesley refers them to Christ:

> Blest, O Israel, art thou,
>   What people is like Thee?
> Saved from sin by Jesus now
>   Thou art, and still shalt be:
> Jesus is thy seven-fold shield,
>   Jesus is thy flaming sword;
> Earth, and hell, and sin shall yield
>   To God's almighty word. (*MHB* 68)

A seemingly less promising example might be, *Jesus, the Conqueror, reigns,* with its strange literal rendering of an obscure Old Testament text: 'Kiss the Son, lest he be angry, and ye perish from the way, when his wrath is kindled but a little' (*Ps* 2:12). Wesley understands this, rightly, in context of the whole psalm — it is about the victory of messiah, the Lord's anointed (v2), his king (v6); and its broad meaning seems to be that his enemies had better sue for peace, for they are fighting against God. There was, of course, an original historical situation that was the psalm's primary reference, but the New Testament refers it to Christ: 'Lord, thou art God..., who by the mouth of thy servant David hast said, Why did the heathen rage, and the people imagine vain things? The kings of the earth stood up, and the rulers were gathered together against the Lord, and against his Christ... thy holy child Jesus, whom thou hast anointed' (*Ac* 4: 24-27). But more, this anointed king is also designated son (v7 of the psalm), and the New Testament cites this also of Jesus, 'as it is also written in the second psalm, Thou art my Son, this day have I begotten thee' (*Ac* 13:33; also *Heb* 1:5; 5:5; cp *Mk* 1:11; 9:7). In light of all this, the psalm may be taken as basic to the New Testament confession of Jesus as Christ and Son of God, and Wesley has an unerring instinct for what the New Testament finds important. He uses the language of the psalm as the New Testament uses it, and 'Kiss the exalted Son' means own him Lord who has been declared Son of God with power. The next lines, 3-6, are direct New Testament language, up to the last two, which echo the psalm again: 'Ask of me, and I shall give thee the heathen for thine inheritance, and the uttermost parts of the earth for thy possession' (v8):

> Extol his kingly power,
> Kiss the exalted Son,
> Who died, and lives to die no more,
> High on his Father's throne:
> Our Advocate with God,
> He undertakes our cause,
> And spreads through all the earth abroad
> The victory of his cross.   (*HP* 262)

This is indeed the psalm, but evangelised — the victory of the cross, quite other than the military victory the psalmist envisaged, yet still Messiah's victory that his psalm was about. Hymnwriter goes far beyond psalmist, but not beyond the psalm and what the Holy Spirit always meant by it. It is enduring scripture and was in God's providence there for the New Testament to use.

We can extend this principle, of the Old Testament adumbrating the New, to other scriptures whose immediate reference was not to Christ but which none the less the New Testament itself refers to Christ — like *Isaiah* 7:14 instanced, which *Matthew* 1:23 quotes as Christian scripture. The New Testament doctrine of Christ takes up the whole messianic history leading to it, and the prophets spoke more than they knew, for its fulfilment was only in Christ to come. That is what the Old Testament was for and about, though the end is not apparent mid-course. Wesley, in such hymns as *Hark! the herald-*

angels sing (as everybody knows it) follows the New Testament itself in reading the New back into the Old, which we may say was waiting for it. Or passing from Christmas to Easter — Wesley, and Samuel Medley (*HP* 196), and of course Handel and the King James translators, are right in declaring:

> I know that my Redeemer lives.

True, we cannot think that Job or the author of the book bearing his name knew anything at all about Christ's resurrection. 'Vindicator' is the undisputed exact translation. But we want none of it in Christian worship! That would be pedantry. Not a word of Handel must be altered: 'I know that my Redeemer liveth, and that he shall stand at the latter day upon the earth; and though worms destroy this body, yet in my flesh shall I see God. For now is Christ risen from the dead, the first fruits of them that sleep'. The Old Testament, and only the Old Testament, is such that it yields Christian meanings before Christ — and that is the true scholarship. Not that we are expected to have all this worked out before we sing the hymns — the Old Testament messiah might actually get in the way of Messiah! But there is depth in Wesley, though the wayfaring man can sing his hymns. We can use them in Christian worship without them being a scholarly exercise, but, hymns apart, Wesley must rank high as an expositor of the Word of God.

One Old Testament text that seems to have been better known to the first Christians than to us is the enigmatic *Deuteronomy* 18:15: 'The Lord thy God will raise up unto thee a Prophet from the mist of thee, of thy brethren, like unto me; unto him ye shall hearken.' It is difficult to think that Moses had some preview of Christ's earthly life, but, coming full circle back to the hymn we began with, we find that Wesley refers the words to Christ, with ample New Testament precedent (*Jn* 1:21,25: 6:14; 7:40; *Ac* 3:22; 7:37):

> Come then, thou Prophet of the Lord,
>   Thou great Interpreter divine;
> Explain thine own transmitted word;
>   To teach , and to inspire is thine:
> Thou only canst thyself reveal,
> Open the book and loose the seal

— that is, only Christ can open the Scriptures, for they are about him and they are his:

> Whate'er the ancient prophets spoke
>   Concerning thee, O Christ, make known;
> Sole Subject of the sacred book,
>   Thou fillest all, and thou alone.   (*WHS* iv.p.136)

In the broad sense we have indicated this is after all true, for Christ is the final reality of Israel's history, all that was prefigured in Abraham, Moses and King David. In him is the unity of Christian Scripture, and all these hymns were written on that understanding. If we quarrel with them our quarrel is not only with them, or with the Old Testament, but with the New. These hymns are scriptural, first to last, and declare the whole word and counsel of God in Christ. No other body of hymns so interprets the Scriptures, so honours Christ.

7. WERE YOU THERE?

Wesley hymns don't read like Negro spirituals, but one celebrated spiritual could provide a heading for very many of them — 'Were you there...?'. Wesley says he was, or rather is — 'there' being the Gospel scene, or all the places in sacred record where God met with his people. He is actually *there*, and participant in events. These hymns are more than a drama of past history, they are his present spiritual experience. He identifies himself with the Bible heroes of faith (as well as with its very great sinners), and only at the most obvious level is this make-believe. He is profoundly one with these people, and he thinks and feels as they thought and felt. Their past lives again in his own vivid present, as he finds the principles of their life, notably the principle of faith, true and valid in his life. In all, it is the same God with whom he has to do.

Faith is the beginning, and Wesley's faith is Abraham's faith, not just propositionally but in the spirit of it, not a set of beliefs but a man believing — Abraham over again:

> The thing surpasses all my thought,
>   But faithful is my Lord;
> Through unbelief I stagger not,
>   For God hath spoke the word.
>
> Faith, mighty faith, the promise sees,
>   And looks to that alone
> Laughs at impossibilities,
>   And cries, It shall be done!   (*WH* 350; *Ro* 4:20f)

And even more explicitly, Wesley *is* Jacob, as he wrestles with God and prevails (*Gen* 32:24-29; *Hos* 12:3f):

> Wrestling, I will not let thee go,
> Till I thy name, thy nature know.
>
> In vain I have not wept, and strove —
> Thy nature, and thy name is LOVE.   (*HP* 434)

He is Moses, too, asking virtually the same thing of God (*Ex* 33:18f):

> Descend, pass by me, and proclaim,
> O Lord of hosts, thy glorious name,
>   The Lord, the gracious Lord,
> Long-suffering, merciful, and kind,
> The God who always bears in mind
>   His everlasting word.   (*MHB* 369)

We too may make such identity of experience ours in these hymns. We can be David, and slay giants (*I Sa:* 17:48f):

> In the strength of God I rise,
>   I run to meet my foe;
> Faith the word of power applies,
>   And lays the giant low:
> Faith in Jesu's conquering name
>   Slings the sin-destroying stone,
> Points the word's unerring aim,
>   And brings the monster down.   (*WH* 269)

Of course, this is imaginative, but faith is not imagination.

Or join Elijah on Carmel at the end of the long drought: *"Behold, there ariseth a little cloud out of the sea, like a man's hand... And it came to pass in the meanwhile , that the heaven was black with clouds and wind, and there was a great rain" (IK* 18:44f). Wesley sees this as the end of a spiritual drought:

> Saw ye not the cloud arise,
>   Little as a human hand?
> Now it spreads along the skies,
>   Hangs o'er all the thirsty land:
> Lo! the promise of a shower
>   Drops already from above;
> But the Lord shall shortly pour
>   All the Spirit of his love.   (*HP* 781)

We are singing of the Evangelical Revival, and please God revival in our time.

Or come now with the prophet to Horeb the mount of God: *'And he said, Go forth and stand upon the mount before the Lord. And behold, the Lord passed by, and a great and strong wind rent the mountains , and brake in pieces the rocks before the Lord; but the Lord was not in the wind: and after the wind an earthquake; but the Lord was not in the earthquake: and after the earthquake a fire; but the Lord was not in the fire: and after the fire a still small voice' (IK* 19:11f). This has become present experience for Wesley, and it can be for us:

> Open, Lord, my inward ear,
>   And bid my heart rejoice!
> Bid my quiet spirit hear
>   Thy comfortable voice:
> Never in the whirlwind found
>   Or where earthquakes rock the place,
> Still and silent is the sound,
>   The whisper of thy grace.

From the world of sin, and noise,
   And hurry, I withdraw;
For the small and inward voice
   I wait with humble awe:
Silent am I now, and still,
   Dare not in thy presence move;
To my waiting soul reveal
   The secret of thy love. (*HP* 540)

Or see the prophet Elisha in the besieged city: '*And when the servant of the man of God was risen early, and gone forth, behold, an host compassed the city both with horses and chariots. And his servant said unto him, "Alas my master! how shall we do?" And he answered, "Fear not: for they that be with us are more than they that be with them". And Elisha prayed, and said, "Lord, I pray thee, open his eyes that he may see". And the Lord opened the eyes of the young man; and he saw: and behold, the mountain was full of horses and chariots of fire round about Elisha"* (IIK 6:15-17):

Though the sons of night blaspheme,
More there are with us than them:
God with us, we cannot fear —
Fear ye fiends, for Christ is here!

Lo, to faith's enlightened sight
All the mountain flames with light;
Hell is nigh, but God is nigher,
Circling us with hosts of fire. (*HP* 811)

This is a good example of how we lose Wesley if we miss his Bible sources. Without the Elisha story, we would be at a loss to make much of these verses. Which mountain — Snowden? Everest? Is it a sunrise? But if we have the story, we can enter into it as Wesley has done. The Bible is like that.

A final Old Testament example, that does not exhaust Wesley's material. We may actually join the three young men in the burning fiery furnace, and find Christ also there (*Dan* 3:24f):

Thee, Son of man, by faith we see,
   And glory in our guide,
Surrounded and upheld by thee
   The fiery test abide. (*MHB* 519)

Figurative, but quite real. The early Methodists were not strangers to mob-attacks and persecution, and we are still not in a world where these things are no more.

And so to the new Testament of our Lord. See how the Gospel record becomes evangelical experience in these hymns. To read Wesley with understanding and a like conviction is to step right inside the Gospel scene:

Now, Lord, to whom for help I call,
    Thy miracles repeat;
With pitying eyes behold me fall
    A leper at thy feet.

Thou seest me deaf to thy commands;
    Open, O Lord my ear;
Bid me stretch out my withered hands,
    And lift them up in prayer.

Silent (alas! thou know'st how long),
    My voice I cannot raise;
But O! when thou shalt loose my tongue
    The dumb shall sing thy praise.

Lame at the pool I still am found;
    Give, and my strength employ;
Light as a hart I then shall bound —
    The lame shall leap for joy.

Blind from my birth to guilt and thee,
    And dark I am within;
The love of God I cannot see,
    The sinfulness of sin.

But thou they say art passing by;
    O let me find thee near;
Jesus, in mercy hear my cry;
    Thou Son of David, hear!   (*WH* 131)

Perhaps it takes Wesley to pass so rapidly from one personation to another, which may limit such a hymn's usefulness for us of slower poetic perceptions. But he is all these people, and he reflects in himself their one need of Jesus. Altogether, he re-experiences these saving encounters, imaging Gospel event as the present event of faith. His identity with these characters is more than a literary device, it is experience like their experience. It is faith-event, of the same stuff as the faith-events of the Gospel, and is real as happening now. Wesley writes from the Gospel and from the heart. It all rests on the persuasion that Jesus Christ is the same yesterday, and today, and for ever.

    And so the Gospel story unfolds, and Wesley is there at each point. He is in the Pharisee's house, and a sinner's words are his words:

    O let me kiss thy bleeding feet,
        And bathe, and wash them with my tears. (*HP* 185; *Lk* 7:37f)

(One word added makes the story of the woman into the story of the cross.) He is in the upper room, at the other feet-washing:

> Wash me, and make me thus thine own;
>   Wash me, and mine thou art;
> Wash me, but not my feet alone,
>   My hands, my head, my heart!   (*MHB* 456; *Jn* 13:9)

(Again the added significant word — my *heart*). Most of all he is at Calvary, an awesome but open place where all may come:

> All ye that pass by,
>   To Jesus draw nigh:
> To you is it nothing that Jesus should die?

(to you so near?) And so the invitation:

> Come, see if there ever was sorrow like his. (*MHB* 188: *Lam* 1:12)

The same:

> Behold him, all ye that pass by,
>   The bleeding Prince of life and peace!
> Come see, ye worms, your Maker die,
>   And say, was ever grief like his?   (*MHB* 186)

We *see* our *Maker* die — which sounds preposterous. But Wesley knows what he is saying. Another tremendous hymn has:

>   that mysterious tree,
> Crucified before our eyes
>   Where we our Maker see.   (*HP* 166)

Other lines of the hymn already quoted, *O Love divine, what hast thou done!*, bring us, in their very crudity, right to foot of the unglamorous cross:

> Pardon for all flows from his side.

> Then let us sit beneath his cross,
>   And gladly catch the healing stream![1]

It is all happening now. The climax of each verse is the same — moving words of Ignatius[2]:

> My Lord, my Love is crucified.

The line keeps coming back remorselessly, with suggestion of the long hours passing as we behold and see. Certainly Wesley was there when they crucified his Lord.

One more such hymn we have already quoted for another reference in it:

> Would Jesus have the sinner die?
> Why hangs he then on yonder tree?

— the cross is but yonder!

> What means that strange expiring cry?

— for our ears have heard it, and

> (Sinners, he prays for you and me)

it is about us:

> 'Forgive them, Father, O forgive!
> They know not that by me they live.'

The central fact of the Christian faith is thus dramatically represented to us — we are addressed as fellow-bystanders at the cross. But this is no mere artifice of words. It is actual experience, and the interest is evangelical. The cross is about the taking away of sin (*Jn* 1:29):

> Dear, loving, all-atoning Lamb,
>   Thee by thy painful agony,
> Thy bloody sweat, thy grief and shame,
>   Thy cross and passion on the tree,
> Thy precious death, and life, I pray —
> Take all, take all my sins away!

This is all by 'yonder tree'. And now again the other story merged into it:

> O let me kiss thy bleeding feet,
>   And bathe, and wash them with my tears,
> The story of thy love repeat
>   In every drooping sinner's ears,
> That all may hear the quickening sound,
>   If I, even I, have mercy found!

The cross is no more drama, but gospel — not spectacle, but faith, and commitment. I (for I understand these hymns only as I enter into them), I am no longer bystander, but believer, and missionary:

> O let thy love my heart constrain,
>   Thy love for every sinner free.

It is the kerygma of the New Testament. I am in the world, not finally of Shakespeare, but of Paul.

But now we greet Christ risen from the dead:

Hail the Lord of earth and heaven!
Praise to thee by both be given;
Thee we greet triumphant now;
Hail the Resurrection thou!   (*Rep Verse* 9 — *HP* 193; *Jn* 11:25)

And we meet the Lord again in the upper room of experience:

Whom now we seek O might we meet!
    Jesus, the crucified,
Shew us thy bleeding hands and feet,
    Thou who for us hast died.

Cause us the record to receive;
    Speak, and the tokens show:
'O be not faithless, but belicve
    In me who died for you."[3]   (*HP* 763; *Jn* 20: 20,27)

So with our Lord's ascension — imaginatively we are 'there' with his disciples:

Master (we will ever say)
Taken from our head today, (*IIK* 2:3,5 AV)
See thy faithful servants, see,
Ever gazing up to thee.   (*Ac* 1:10)

But more than pious fancy, this is real now as we seek the things above where Christ is:

Grant, though parted from our sight
High above yon azure height,   (*Lk* 24:51)
Grant our hearts may thither rise ,
Following thee beyond the skies.   (*Rep Verse* 10 — *HP* 197; *Col* 3:1)

And so through to Pentecost — we are there too, or rather Pentecost is here:

The Spirit is come,
The Witness of Jesus returned to his home. (*HP* 296)

.   .   .   .   .

Our Jesus is gone up on high,
    For us the blessing to receive;
It now comes streaming from the sky,
    The Spirit comes and sinners live.[4]

57

— yes, now. This is historic Christianity in the present of real experience. It must be so, if it is true.

NOTES

1.   *HP* emendation of this (175) is warranted:
   > Then let us stand beneath the cross ,
   > And feel his love a healing stream.

   They were not followers of Jesus who sat watching him suffer (*Mt* 27:36; contrast *Jn* 19:25f). And the amended second line, after Watts ('Sorrow and love flow mingled down), may better reflect the Gospel reticence.

2.   'Amor meus crucifixus est', as current from the Middle Ages. (For note on Greek original, *Companion to HP*, p 130). John Mason, *Spiritual Songs,* 1683, strengthened it with the title 'Lord':
   > My Lord, my Love, was crucified.

   John Wesley (*HP* 568) took this, only restoring the vivid Ignatian present-time, and that is the line Charles used for his refrain. He had already used the exact four words in a hymn:
   > My Love is crucified.   *(WH 26)*

3.   This ought to be classified in hymn-books as an Easter hymn. Wesley has plenty more fellowship hymns.

4.   Earlier verse in original of *HP* 307.

8. WRESTLING JACOB[1]

After Calvary, no scene in all Scripture so held Charles Wesley's evangelical imagination as did Jacob's encounter at the Jabbok ford. He often preached about it — Telford[2] lists eight Journal references, beginning May 24th, 1741: 'I preached on Jacob's wrestling for the blessing. Many, then, I believe, took hold on his strength, and will not let him go, till he bless them, and tell them his name.' It must have been powerful preaching, in the very strength that was its subject. But in verse Wesley goes even further, for he here identifies himself, imaginatively but also seriously and believingly, with Jacob. He *is* that man, in immediate real experience.

His earliest such verses, in terms and tone virtually identical with the sermon, take Jacob's words on to his own lips: 'I will not let thee go, except thou bless me' (*Gen* 32:26):

> The blessing of thy love bestow,
>   For this my cries shall never fail;
> Wrestling, I will not let thee go,
>   I will not, till my suit prevail.   (*WH* 149)

. . . . .

> Lord, I will not let thee go,
> Till THE BLESSING thou bestow;
> Hear my Advocate divine;
> Lo! to his my suit I join;
> Joined to his it cannot fail;
> Bless me, for I *will* prevail.   (*WH* 379)

These are from the important Pt II of *Hymns and Sacred Poems* 1739. This second part, headed by *Where shall my wondering soul begin?*, sounds a new personal and evangelical note. Its hymns we may take to be first expressions in verse of the new experience the Wesley brothers had so recently entered into. So that Wrestling Jacob goes back, in effect autobiographically, to Charles's earliest evangelical days. Thereafter, it is a recurring theme.[3] WRESTLING JACOB proper comes three years later, 1742.

This Jacob motif comes into some of Wesley's finest hymns:

> I hold thee with a trembling hand,
>   I will not let thee go
> Till steadfastly by faith I stand,
>   And all thy goodness know.   (*HP* 740 — 1740)

. . . . .

The spirit of interceding grace
  Give us in faith to claim,
To wrestle till we see thy face,
  And know thy hidden name.

Till thou the perfect love impart,
  Till thou thyself bestow,
Be this the cry of every heart:
  I will not let thee go!

I will not let thee go, unless
  Thou tell thy name to me,
With all thy great salvation bless,
  And make me all like thee. (*HP* 558 — 1749)

Such are generally holiness hymns, and it is right they should be — holiness comes of encounter with God. But *the* hymn does not get that far — in it, we stay with Jacob at Jabbok ford. This is not yet about the image of God in his children, but simply the evangelical love of God to sinners.

Who is Wrestling Jacob? — the man Jacob to begin with, and also, he being Patriarch, his descendant people, still bearing his name and character. This is implied in the original by his new racial name *Israel* (*Gen* 32:28), and is the interpretation in Hosea's prophecy, where Jacob the Lord's people is he who strove with God (12:2-4). Wesley, who is aware of what the prophet has written,[4] goes back to Jacob the man. Or rather, he comes forward to Jacob of the new covenant, Christian man, who asks,

Art thou the Man that died for me?

More than a poet's fancy, this is a believer's profound appropriation of Scripture. The original Jacob encountered a mysterious but gracious God, and prevailed with him. Wesley's Jacob, who is Wesley, encounters God-man, and prevails with *him*. We read Wrestling Jacob from the New Testament, and reach a Christian end of the story. For but one of Jacob's prayers was granted — he gained the blessing, but was not told the divine name. New Jacob makes the two prayers in one:

Speak to my heart, in blessings speak...
And tell me if thy name is LOVE.

And he is told — the new name, before Christ unutterable:

Thy nature, and thy name is LOVE.

And our ears are blessed beyond the desire of many prophets and kings and righteous men, and patriarchs.

WRESTLING JACOB, as Dr. Rattenbury discerningly pointed out,[5] is Wesley's evangelical variant of a celebrated theme of the mystics — the Dark Night of the Soul; and he sets Wesley's beside a hymn of this latter title by St. John of the Cross:[6]

> Oh, night, that led me, guiding night,
> Oh night far sweeter than the dawn:
> Oh, night, that did so then unite
> The Loved with his Beloved,
> Transforming Lover in Beloved.

The difference is absolute, and means another religion. Essentially it is between two sorts or conceptions of love — eros and *agape*, the aesthetic and *the evangelical*, love I find in me and love that *comes to me*, love that is contemplation and love that is *grace*.

Wesley's setting, too, is night — suggested rather than described, to be sensed more in retrospect when at last the morning shall break. It is dark night — I cannot see the One I still hold on to now that my companions have gone on across the ford and left me, humanly alone. None knows better than Wesley the New Testament meaning of fellowship, but he knows too that for each in the fellowship there was a primary direct meeting with God. There is an aloneness of evangelical experience, especially at its inception. Alone then with the unknown Other, I now address him: 'Come!'

It might seem that my word begins the encounter, as it does the poem. But not so; I can converse with him only because he *has come*, to me. His coming was the true beginning, just before the poem begins. This first word says the first thing I can possibly know about God, he *comes* to me. I can make inferences about the Creator, but not certainly, and not personally. He is yet unknown to me, and only by meeting him can I know him, and I cannot meet him until he comes to me:

> Come, O thou Traveller unknown.

There is an advent in Christian experience corresponding to *the Advent* — he comes now to me, so that my experience rests upon the revelation of God. It is not my soul's dark night, or any subjective state, that gains the blessing, but he who, coming, brings it.

Night itself has no mystic charm for Jacob, is but the dramatic background, almost Shakespearean, to darker night within:

> I need not tell thee who I am,
> My misery or sin declare

— it is a sinner that wrestles with God, like first Jacob. So at once the evangelical appeal, not to any love that is mine, but altogether to love that is of him, as yet the only Lover. He has called me by my name before I know his:

> Thyself hast called me by my name,
> Look on thy hands, and read it there.

But the other way round — How can *I* know *his* name?

> But who, I ask thee, who art thou?
> Tell me thy name, and tell me now.

There is no way of my knowing till he does tell me, no esoteric knowledge already mine; but the one mysticism is the mystery of grace, the evangelical love of God:

> Art thou the Man that died for me?
> The secret of thy love unfold.

The secret is his name of Love. The whole hymn, a prayer, is comprehended in a single petition,

> Tell me thy name,

and its answer:

> Thy nature, and thy name is LOVE.

The prayer is wrestling prayer, but the initiative was never mine but his all along who first came to me. Nor shall the issue rest with me — it is not *that* I wrestle but *with whom* that shall decide.

> When I am weak, then I am strong

is Jacob's great paradox — Paul's actually (*II Co*: 12:10), lifted bodily in surely literature's most unerring transference of thought and language from one man to another:[7]

> And

(adding finality even to that)

> when my all of strength shall fail,
> I shall with the God-man prevail.

There is clear evangelical reason for the paradox. If I have no strength left, then necessarily the issue rests with the Other. That I none the less prevail is because of who this Other is — the Man that died for me, God-man.

> My prayer hath power with God

— but not because the prayer is powerful, still less I who pray; only because he to whom I pray is God of grace unspeakable. Instant prayer — mere, importunate asking, when all I can do is ask — will conquer only the God of grace.

> In vain I have not wept,[8] and strove

— but it would have been vain with any other sort of God, or with God on any other terms. My determination, wrestling, not to let him go would be Arminian, but not Pelagian — far more nearly Calvinist than at all Pelagian. I can spare my breath and moral effort unless God, his nature and very name, is Love. And this he only can tell me, love understood in the Gospel being his grace to me, and so the knowledge of it the revelation of himself. The new, unutterable name can only be disclosed to me, by him who bears it. To know his name is my prayer, and he grants the prayer because of what his name is. When I say to him,

> I know thee ... who thou art

emphasis is all away from me and my knowing (though indeed I know), and all on him, who he is. I know him because he is evangelically known, my Saviour,

> Jesus, the feeble sinner's friend.

Not by mystical insight but

> Through faith

— which answers to the revelation of God —

> I see thee face to face,
> I see thee face to face, and live.

The struggle, being graciously determined, issues not in some deeper realisation of eros in the soul but in the revelation to the soul of the *agape* of God, his very name of Love:

> 'Tis Love! 'tis Love! thou diedst for me.

Of myself, I am all helplessness, all weakness. My nature's strength withered, I depend on God alone for strength, and have no power even to move from him (did an Arminian say that?)
    This love comes to me, even as day comes. Not so the other love, in night far sweeter than the dawn. That was an entering into the night, and dawn was to come only as an interruption to love. But the love was not *agape*. *Agape comes,* a gospel dawn. The wrestling was till the break of day, and the

prevalence of Jacob's prayer is only now, as indeed day breaks. The dark night has revealed nothing and the struggle has availed nothing, until at last

> The morning breaks, the shadows flee,

and I can see God and say to him:

> Pure, UNIVERSAL LOVE thou art.

This is by definition Arminian — such is God's love:

> To me, to all thy bowels move;
> Thy nature, and thy name is LOVE.

But his whole account of this love coming to a man is as decisively Calvinist: only God makes it morning, and that is how his love comes:

> The Sun of Righteousness on me
> Hath rose, with healing in his wings.   (*Gen* 32:31; *Mal* 4:2)[9]

Jacob did not make the sun rise, it rose on Jacob. And the rest is God's day:

> Nor wilt thou with the night depart,
> But stay, and love me to the end.

This is experimental religion, but first it is revealed religion: not my sight is determinative but God's light — the light of the Gospel. His whisper I hear in my heart ('I died for thee') is his historic word, though he does immediately say it to me. I can wrestle through unending night for ever (or if I could!) but will never, till I am told, in the last analysis *till he tells me*, know God-man who died for me.

This classic of the soul is one of the great theological hymns — an exposition of evangelical Christianity, so often misunderstood, sometimes misunderstanding itself, as being strong on feeling and weak on doctrine. The hymn, being a personal prayer, is of course about the one who prays, but more importantly is about God who answers his prayer. It is grace, as of the morning, that gives the answer; not spirituality, as of the night, that obtained it. Spirituality has collapsed, and it is at this point of collapse, where Wesley's all of strength has failed, that he prevails with God. We may speak of *evangelical spirituality*, but then all is of God. The central paradox is finally of the divine objective centre to personal faith, the insight that is revelation, the grace by which we lay hold on God, the love we feel that is God's love to us, the experience that is ours because the election was always his — always the fundamental *I*, always the most fundamental *thou*.

For Jacob say Paul, and you are at the heart of this hymn. Christ's enemy made Christian against his will, he has been apprehended by Christ Jesus that he might testify the gospel of the grace of God — 'Calvinist' if that is

Calvinism. 'And he hath said unto me, my grace is sufficient for thee: for my power is made perfect in weakness. Most gladly therefore will I glory in my weakness, that the power of Christ may rest upon me ... for when I am weak, then am I strong' (*II Co* 12:9f). Not only these classic end-words that Wesley has put into his hymn, but the whole passage (we might say, this whole epistle) interprets for him the strange Genesis original. Jabbok ford is his Damascus road, the place of Christ-encounter. Once there, a man is never the same again:

> Contented now upon my thigh
>   I halt, till life's short journey end;
> All helplessness, all weakness, I
>   On thee alone for strength depend:
> Nor have I power from thee to move:
> Thy nature, and thy name is LOVE.

> Lame as I am I take the prey,
>   Hell, earth, and sin with ease o'ercome;
> I leap for joy, pursue my way,
>   And as a bounding hart fly home,
> Through all eternity to prove
> Thy nature, and thy name is LOVE.

NOTES

1. *Hymns and Sacred Poems* 1742, in 14 verses. *Rep Verse* 25 in full. John, 1780, omitted the two dispensable verses, and *HP* still has the twelve (in one solid block, ensuring they will never be sung!)
2. J. Telford, *New MHB Illustrated*, p.181.
3. *WH* has references in sixteen hymns: 17:11; 109:1,2; 124:6; 136 ('WRESTLING JACOB'); 138:3,4; 145:5; 149:5; 158:3; 288:3-5; 333:3; 351:2; 369:5; 379:3; 424:6; 515:6; 516:4.
4. 'In vain I have not wept, and strove' — *wept* is Hosea's word, not in Genesis original.
5. J.E. Rattenbury, *Wesley's Legacy to the World*, p 128f.
6. Tr, G. Cunningham Graham.
7. This link with the *Corinthians* passage Wesley owes to Matthew Henry: 'Wrestling believers may obtain glorious victories, and yet come off with broken bones; for "when they are weak, then are they strong" — weak in themselves, but strong in Christ.' But the hymn goes beyond this generalised statement to Wesley's personal identification in experience with both patriarch and apostle.
8. *Hos* 12:4. Not stated in *Genesis*, this seems dramatically right and intrinsically likely. Is it fanciful to follow right through from ford to garden, to the prayers and supplications and strong crying and tears (*Heb* 5:7) of him who became Jacob for us, the progenitor of New Israel?

9. The link with other scripture is this time directly Wesley's — 'The Sun of Righteousness shall arise with healing in his wings' (*Mal* 4:2). Henry's comment, ' it is sunrise with that soul that has communion with God', does not go outside the *Genesis* story (v 31). And once more it is Wesley who so personalizes it all — 'on me', 'my soul'.

(Reproduced from *The Evangelical Magazine*, with kind approval of the Paternoster Press.)

9. ON THE EDGE OF CALVINISM (1)

We are to look through Charles Wesley's eyes at a most difficult, finally mysterious, but essential, and glorious part of evangelical doctrine. It is the whole matter of the grace by which we are saved — its extent (for all?), and its relation to the human will. Wesley gave the Arminian answers to these questions, and had strong things to say about Calvinists. But he was more Calvinist than he knew. 'The true gospel', his brother once declared,[1] 'touches the very edge of Calvinism.'

Calvinists tend to find in all Arminianism an incipient *Pelagianism*, and will even use the terms interchangeably. The argument is that by the Arminian scheme it is we finally who say whether we are to be saved. But then, Calvinism followed through in that way cannot stop short of the antinomian opposite heresy, and in the end fatalism, for by it we neither need do anything about our salvation, nor can. It is not fair to judge either system by its caricature, by whatever reasoning arrived at. We must recognise at the outset that neither is a logically ultimate position, for Calvinism does insist on accountability, and Arminianism does affirm grace.

Wesley begins where Augustine and the Reformers began — firmly with the doctrine of grace, that Pelagius knew nothing about:

> He made it possible for all
>   To turn again, and live;
> And therefore doth his gospel call
>   And his good spirit strive.

> Through grace we hearken to thy voice ---. (*Works* iii, p 65)

He made possible what was never otherwise a possibility, and *by grace* we hearken — like Lydia, 'whose heart the Lord opened, to give heed---' (*Ac* 16:14). 'For all' is Arminian, but with the insistence we really *hear* the gospel only through grace, which is then the prior condition of any response. In words of another hymn:

> A power to choose, a will to obey,
>   Freely his grace *restores*;
> We all may find the living way
>   And call the Saviour ours. (*Works* i, p 311)

The italics, Wesley's, bring out the key-word — fallen man has lost his moral will, and only grace can *restore* it. This is free, and we have made no initial deposit. Wesley is thus highly Calvinist before he starts being Arminian, with his 'all may'. A universal offer is hardly Calvinism, but prevenient grace is.

By definition of prevenience, grace is sovereign — 'thy grand prerogative', in noble words of our greatest Calvinist hymn:[2]

> And none shall in the honour share.

And it seems none but Calvinists shall share the honour of saying so! But no — this is Wesley language, too:

> What shall I do my God to love,
>   My loving God to praise,
> The length, and breadth, and height to prove,
>   And depth of sovereign grace!

The divine sovereignty means the total initiative of God, and Wesley feels he is spectator to his very experience of grace:

> In Christ abundantly forgiven,
>   I see thy mercies rise.

He makes the Arminian inference from this:

> Thy sovereign grace to all extends ---
>   Or it had passed by me. (*HP* 46)

But it is the sovereign divine action he is talking about. We might say that Wesley is an Arminian evangelist with the Calvinist explanation of his own state of grace. The two are one in an evangelism of experience:

> O let me kiss thy bleeding feet,
>   And bathe, and wash them with my tears,
> The story of thy love repeat
>   In every drooping sinner's ears,
> That all may hear the quickening sound,
> If I, even I, have mercy found.

'Or it had passed by me' — it is the same evangelical reasoning, from sovereign grace, or love, to universal proclamation:

> O let thy love my heart constrain,
>   Thy love for every sinner free,
> That every fallen soul of man
>   May taste the grace that found out me,
> That all mankind, with me, may prove
> Thy sovereign, everlasting love. (*HP* 185)

No doubt that last line has controversial overtones, the hymn coming whence it came in the first of two anti-Calvinist tracts of *Hymns on God's Everlasting Love*, 1741, when feeling was at its height. There must have been enough of the natural man in both brothers[3] to enjoy turning the language of their theological opponents back on themselves, as politicians do! But it is none the less from his heart. Because he owes his experience to the love that is grace, and not to anything that was in him to begin with, he can quite seriously speak of that love, that grace, as sovereign. It is all thoroughly evangelical in principle, and in no wise Pelagian. A doctrine of grace that no Calvinist need quarrel with is its basis.

But what is Wesley saying? Sovereign grace or love for all — is not this the theological formula for universal salvation? Again logically, it might seem so, but logic or no logic Wesley is not a Universalist.

At least *evangelical* Arminians (but properly, are there other?) join with Calvinists, as historically the Wesley brothers joined with Whitefield, in preaching a gospel the response to which has eternal consequence.

As to Wesley, this has been questioned. Ernest Rattenbury argued[4]: 'Since the words "universal salvation" seem to tremble on the lips of Wesley, even if he never actually used them, may not his sons legitimately entertain the larger hope?' But his supporting references are not quite to the point. They are to *penitential* hymns, as he notes:

> But I surely shall feel,
> Ere I drop into hell,
> That the arms of thy love are beneath. (*Works* iv, p 413)

. . . . .

And if I am lost, to be lost in thy love. (*Works* iv, p 416)

Such lines are surely about *assurance of salvation* to a penitent. To say that such will never be lost is not to say that all will ever repent. And the concept of perdition in these hymns is real. Dr. Rattenbury might better have supported his case from the *Hymns on God's Everlasting Love*, which are at Wesley's furthest remove from Calvinism and do at times come near saying 'universal salvation':

> Enlarge my heart to all mankind,
>   The purchase of thy dying groans;
> O let me by this token find
>   They all are thy redeeméd ones:
> For if I loved whom God abhorred,
> The servant were above his Lord. (*Works* iii, p 29)

. . . . .

> Low at thy throne of love I bow,
> Of universal love. (*Works* iii, p 63)

This is universal salvation, surely? Nearly, but not quite! It is precisely his Arminian persuasion of real and ultimate choice that keeps Wesley from making the equation. These lines are from the same source, imaginatively on reprobate lips[5]:

> I this record leave behind —
> Though damned, I was forgiven. (*Works* iii, p 15)

>   .   .   .   .   .

> Though I am damned, yet God is love. (*Works* iii, p 27)

All have been redeemed, are actually forgiven — and some are in hell! This is heightened language, but Wesley is distinguishing between a universal atonement, which he does find (and is to be found) in Scripture, and universal salvation, which, Dr. Rattenbury concedes, he never affirms (nor Scripture).

It is this positive and negative combined — universal atonement, but not necessary and universal salvation — that give so many of these hymns their poignancy, even tragic sense:

> Nay, but his bowels yearned to see
>   The people hungry, scattered, faint;
> Nay, but he uttered over thee,
>   Jerusalem, a true complaint —
> Jerusalem, who shedd'st his blood,
> That with his tears for thee hath flowed.
>
> He wept, because thou *wouldst* not see
>   The grace which sure salvation brings;
> How oft would he have gathered thee,
>   And cherished underneath his wings:
> But thou wouldst not — unhappy thou!
> And justly art thou hardened now.[6]

Wesley was never a Universalist, though we may speculate he would have liked to be — so would Jesus when he wept over Jerusalem. But as firmly as any Calvinist, but with more pathos (but what about Whitefield?), he accepts that all will not be saved. Yet there is nothing harsh or threatening in these hymns. Rather, it is the dread possibility of rejecting the gospel, to our eternal loss, that gives them their passion and urgency:

> Sinners, turn; why will ye die?
> God, your Maker, asks you why:
> God, who did your being give,
> Made you with himself to live:
> He the fatal cause demands,
> Asks the work of his own hands,
> Why, ye thankless creatures, why
> Will ye cross his love, and die?

The hymn goes on:

> God, your Saviour, asks you why,

> God the Spirit asks you why.

Sixteen verses press the question, varied slightly but with each time the dread end-word 'die', down to the final:

> Why will you resolve to die?   (*WH* 6-8 — *MHB* 327)

Ezekiel prophesies again: 'Why will ye die, O house of Israel?' (19:31, which heads the hymn).

This preaching is first Wesley's own evangelical experience, which has left him no room for boasting or excuse, or complacency:

> How have I thy Spirit grieved,
>   Since first with me he strove!
> Obstinately disbelieved,
>   And trampled on thy love!
> I have sinned against the light,
>   I have broke from thy embrace;
> No, I would not, when I might,
>   Be freely saved by grace!   (*WH* 175)

>   .   .   .   .

> All the hindrance is in me,
>   Thou ready art to save;
> But I would not come to thee,
>   That I thy life may have:
> Stubborn and rebellious still,
>   From thy arms of love I fly;
> Yes, I will be lost; I will,
>   In spite of mercy, die.

This is a further echo of the *Ezekiel* text, and it seems a true exposition. And perhaps Calvinists can see how, in Arminian terms, Wesley points it to a God-honouring conclusion:

> Holy, meek, and gentle Lamb,
>   With me what canst thou do?
> Though thou leav'st me as I am,
>   I own three good and true:
> Thou wouldst have me life embrace,
>   Thou for me and all wast slain;
> Thou hast offered me thy grace,
>   'Twas I that made it vain.   (*Works* iii, p 10)

That is the clear Arminian position. Christ died for all, and offers grace to all — but I can still make it vain. Can man make the grace of God vain? A man can *as far as he is concerned* — 'yes' in that sense. Paul thought so: 'we entreat also, that ye receive not the grace of God in vain' (*II Co* 6:1).

Wesley, then, is neither Pelagian nor Universalist, but evangelical, and that does put him with Calvinists on one side of a main dividing line. What, then, separated him from them? In my further paper on the Calvinist-Arminian issue I shall argue Wesley's considerable affinity with the Calvinists. It is important first to recognise the real differences, being two: his theological difference with Calvinism proper, and his further, ethical, difference with the debased hyper-Calvinism he actually encountered.

What had he at issue with *Calvinism*, leaving out the distortions? There was no doubt what in Wesley's mind — and it will surprise Calvinists! Calvinism asserts at all costs the honour of God — 'Let God be true, and every man a liar'. He would defend *God's honour*, against Calvinists! Mark the front on which he attacks. He is not, or not first, in liberal vein, defending the spirit of man against a system that degrades man. He is defending the good name of God, reverently by appeal to the Word of God.

Hymns on God's Everlasting Love, to which Charles Wesley largely contributed, is positively Arminian, with fine evangelistic hymns like 'Would Jesus have the sinner die?' and 'Let earth and heaven agree'. The rest is provocatively anti-Calvinist, its author having been first provoked by the Calvinist teaching. 'THE HORRIBLE DECREE'[7] screams its indignation in solid italic, within self-indemnifying quotation-marks:

> 'Sinners, abhor the fiend,
>   His other gospel hear:
> *The God of truth did not intend*
>   *The thing his words declare:*
>   *He offers grace to all*
>   *Which most cannot embrace —*
> *Mocked with an ineffectual call*
>   *And insufficient grace.*

> *The righteous God consigned*
> *Them over to their doom,*
> *And sent the Saviour of mankind*
> *To damn them from the womb,*
> *To damn for falling short*
> *Of what they could not do,*
> *For not believing the report*
> *Of that which was not true.*

But then,

> *'He did not damn them — but decreed*
> *They never should be saved.'*

Brilliant satire, this, but to the serious end of honouring God:

> Satanic sophistry!
> But still, all-gracious God,
> They charge the sinner's death on thee,
> Who bought'st him with thy blood.   (*Works* iii, p 35f)

Such is the 'horrible decree' — pure blasphemy, with Wesley at pains to show it is not he saying it.   Other 'hymns' have just the note of personal testimony, but their tone is still strident, and they seem dramatically overdone — they belong here rather than with his main devotional verse:

> Thou hast reprobated none,
>   Thou from *Pharuoh's* blood art free;
> Thou didst once for all atone —
>   *Judas, Esau, Cain*, and me.   (*Works* iii, p 31)

.   .   .   .   .

> If grace to me doth still abound,
> Then *Judas* might have pardon found.   (*Works* iii, p 43)

(Note 'might have' — not the suggestion he did, or would hereafter. Again, Wesley is not a Universalist.)

Controversial writing, however cogent its author may feel it to be, seldom registers with other than partisans, and Wesley can be no exception. The Calvinists must have been pretty immune to all this. Their answer would be bluntly that Wesley is altogether too solicitous for God's honour. Limited atonement being in fact the doctrine, all Wesley's fuming, and even self-deprecation, is beside the Scripture point — we honour God as we submit to his revealed word. But *is* limitation — of grace, that is — the Bible doctrine? Sufficient scripture says *not*. Ezekiel we saw: 'Why will ye die, O house of Israel? For I have no pleasure in the death of him that dieth, saith the Lord

God: wherefore turn yourselves, and live' (18:31f). And in universal terms of the New Testament: 'God our Saviour --- willeth that all men should be saved, and come to the knowledge of the truth' (*I Ti* 2:3-6; also 4:10 and *Tit* 2:11). Calvinist embarrassment at these Pastoral texts is illustrated by Hendriksen's special pleading that 'all' in these places does not mean simply *all*.[8] He would not thus reduce the 'all' of *Romans* 3:23, and these too are doctrinal universals of the New Testament — likewise *II Peter* 3:9. Calvinists also must be humble before the Word of God, and Wesley's valid point is that the New Testament does present God's universal offer of grace, and if this is not true we make God insincere.

Scripture validates, not importantly Wesley's protest verse, but importantly his great evangelistic hymns of the Revival, that Bible Christians need not scruple to sing. They echo Paul's field-preaching, that God 'commandeth all men everywhere to repent' (*Ac* 17:30):

> Plenteous he is in truth and grace,
> He wills that all the fallen race
>   Should turn, repent, and live:
> His pardoning grace for all is free —
> Transgression, sin, iniquity
>   He freely doth forgive.   (*MHS* 369)

.   .   .   .   .

> Whose mercy is divinely free,
> For all the fallen race, and me.   (*HP* 47)

.   .   .   .

> For all my Lord was crucified;
> For all, for all my Saviour died.   (*HP* 226)

———————————

But Wesley's controversy was not only with true Calvinism but with its antinomian distortion (so unlike Calvin!). This has a confident doctrine of assurance, but seems to imply some strange exegesis of Scripture; as —

> 'In part perhaps you may,
>   You cannot wholly fall,
> Cannot become a castaway
>   Like *non-elected Paul*. (*I Co* 9:27 AV)

> 'God sees in you no sin,
>   On his decree depend;
> (the smug other side to the 'horrible decree')
> You who did in the Spirit begin
> In flesh can never end. (*Gal* 3:3)

74

'If once the spirit unclean
    Out of his house is gone,
He never more can enter in,
    Or seize you for his own:
    You need not dread the fate
    Of reprobates accurst,
Or tremble lest your last estate
    Be worse than was the first.'   (*Works* iii, p 48f — *Mt* 12:43-45)

It is all the same metre as the other pungent verses noted — double-short, Wesley's militant metre, of 'Soldiers of Christ' fame, his weapon here of heavy sarcasm.

In fairness, he can be sarcastic about himself, recalling how, not all that time ago, he had listened to just these insinuations of 'the fiend', with further novel interpretations of Scripture resulting:

    I listened to a lie
    Which nature liked so well,
Believed the soothing fiend, that I
    Could never fall — and fell.   (*ICo* 10:12)

    One of the happy sect
    Who scoff at mourners poor,   (*Matt* 5:4)
That will not dream themselves elect
    Till they have made it sure.   (*Works* iii, p 52f — *II Pe* 1:10)

It is hard to believe this had ever seriously been Wesley's position, but he did admit it very nearly had been: 'I was once on the brink of antinomianism, by unwarily reading Crisp and Saltmarsh. Just then warm in my first love, I was in the utmost danger when Providence threw in my way Baxter's treatise, entitled, An Hundred Errors of Dr. Crisp demonstrated'.[9]

That such verses, about others and about Wesley himself, are not figments but describe with some accuracy views actually then current may be judged from a few of the quotations Fletcher made from the notorious Dr. Tobias Crisp referred to: 'Must not a believer, an elect, be reckoned to be a sinner while he does sin? No. Though he does sin, yet he is not reckoned as a sinner, his sins are reckoned to be taken away from him.' 'There is no condition in the covenant of grace; man has no tie upon him to perform anything whatsoever, as a condition that must be observed on his part; and there is not one bond or obligation on man to the fulfilling of his part in the covenant, or partaking of the benefits of it.' 'Must they now labour to gain these things, as if it were referred to their well or evil walking; that as they walk, so shall they speed? The Lord does nothing in his people upon conditions.' 'Every elect vessel, from the first instant of his being, is as pure in the eyes of God from the charge of sin, as he shall be in glory.' 'There is as much ground to be confident of the pardon of sin to a believer, so soon as he committed it, as to believe it after he has performed all the humiliation in the world: a believer may be assured of pardon as soon as he commits any sin, even adultery and murder.' 'God does no longer stand displeased, though a believer do sin often.' 'There is no sin that ever believers commit that can possibly do them any hurt.'[10] Nor are these the oddities of a mere eccentric, soon to be forgotten. Crisp's sermons, seventeenth-century, were remembered and influential through most of the eighteenth. As late as the seventeen-seventies Richard Hill, in an extraordinary book, *The Finishing Stroke*, was as uninhibited in saying the same things. Certainly when Wesley wrote his satires, thirty years before, he was confronting a real enemy. But this was never the true Calvinism, and Fletcher was scrupulously fair to make the distinction, as we must be: 'I confess that these branches of Dr. Crisp's doctrine which stand in direct opposition to the practical gospel of Christ, I have taken the liberty to call Crispianity; for had I called them Christianity, my conscience and one half of the Bible would have flown in my face: and had I called them Calvinism, Williams, Flavel, Alleine, Bishop Hopkins, and numbers of sound Calvinists, would have proved me mistaken.'[11]

All the same, it must be understood that Wesley's satires were directed not only against the Antinomian distortion, but comprehensively against Calvinism. Even the 'sound Calvinists' were committed to the theory (Bible doctrine it is not) of limited atonement, and this, Wesley devastatingly shows, does despite to much Scripture, and calls in question the character of God.

NOTES

1. Minutes of Conference, 1745.
2. 'Great God of wonders', Samuel Davies.
3. Cp John (*HP* 520):
   > *Sufficient, sovereign, saving grace.*
   (This, opening hymn of the first pamphlet, I attribute to him, following Bett.)
4. J.E. Rattenbury: *The Evangelical Doctrines of Charles Wesley's Hymns*, p 173.
5. There is, of course, highest precedent for this device — *Lk* 16:23-30.
6. *Lk* 13:34; 19:41. Earlier verses of hymn already quoted (*HP* 185). Cp John, further verses of his hymn quoted (*HP* 520):
   > For those that *will not come* to him
   > The ransom of his life was paid.

   > The Lamb for every castaway,
   > For every soul of man was slain.
7. Wesley's ironic title is Calvin rather misleadingly Englished: 'decretum quidem horribile fateor'. 'Horribile' : *dreadful*, in older sense of *to be dreaded, had in awe.*
8. *The Epistles of Timothy and Titus*, p 93. His analogies are surprisingly weak. Obviously in *Mk* 11:32 and the four like instances adduced, 'all' has simple local reference — everybody there at the time. But these Pastoral

texts are doctrinal, and having nothing to do with particular situations and mere physical proximity.

9. Letter to John Fletcher, quoted in *Third Check to Antinomianism* (*Five Checks*, 1872 ed. i, p 271).
10. Fletcher : *Second Check* (i, pp 163-5).
11. Fletcher : *Third Check* (i, p 281).

10. ON THE EDGE OF CALVINISM (2)

Our discussion so far has been of Wesley's Arminianism, for which he found scriptural support — God wills all men to be saved, and commands all men everywhere to repent. Most of the rest is about Calvinism — Wesley's fear and avoidance of its doctrines, but its profound reality in the religion of his greatest hymns.

The cardinal Calvinist doctrine is *election*, and this is a cardinal doctrine of scripture. 'The election of grace', Paul calls it (*Ro* 11:5): 'even as he chose us in him before the foundation of the world, that we should be holy and without blemish before him in love: having foreordained us unto adoption as sons through Jesus Christ unto himself, according to the good pleasure of his will, to the praise of the glory of his grace, which he freely bestowed on us in the Beloved: in whom we have our redemption through his blood, the forgiveness of our trespasses, according to the riches of his grace; (*Eph* 1:4-7). 'Grace', repeated, is the great and comprehensive word, and election is inalienably part of the doctrine.

Yet Paul does not work out a doctrine of negative-election, to reprobation. He has no corresponding opposite of such a passage as this, but his message is positively grace. Electing grace was how he saw the success of the Gospel — 'knowing, brethren beloved of God, your election' (*I Thess* 1:4); notwithstanding that his actual mission preaching had been the call to all men to repent (*Ac* 17:30). Dating as far back as around AD50, the Thessalonian letters are windows into the first evangelism — the Gospel precisely *came* (*I Thess* 1:5), to places of the Holy Spirit's choosing (*Ac* 16: 6-10). As it historically happened, it was a special providence by which these people became God's people — indeed by repenting and turning from idols to God (*I Thess* 1:9). It all confirmed Paul's doctrine of a gracious election. This is what Arminians must come to terms with.

But can they possibly? Election in grace and a universal offer of grace seem a sheer logical contradiction. But the evangelical Arminian can begin to see it if he considers his actual Christian experience, and that *must* go back to the grace of God. If I am a child of God, it is because God first willed this. At some point was God's call and my response, but the two were one divine operation. I might have said 'No' to God (or I would have been an automaton and never a son), but the Holy Spirit was in my 'Yes'. Paradox remains, but only because I can never explain the work of the Spirit of God within my spirit. When I trace my Christian beginnings, I can go back only so far, and before that is God. It is the word of God that is at work in us who believe, as we believe (*I Thess* 2:13), and I have little difficulty in calling this election, and far more difficulty in calling it anything else.

Now Wesley knows nothing of election, or does not think he does. He mostly avoids the term, and his occasional attempts to Arminianise it can only be judged perverse — like this exposition of *Romans* 8:29:

78

> Whom his eternal mind *foreknew*,
>   That they the power would use,
>   Ascribe to God the glory due,
>   And not his grace refuse.

> Them, only them, his will *decreed*,
>   Them did he *choose* alone ---.

> Them, *the elect* consenting few,
>   Who yield to proffered love ---.   (*Works* i, pp 311-2)

These verses immediately follow and take up 'A power to choose' (quoted, first paper), but he is less at ease now in trying to accommodate this to election, that might threaten it. He redefines election as consent, which simply upends the straightforward New Testament, indeed dictionary, meaning of the word. It is a word he finds hard to bring to his lips, and harder to use with any conviction. It never comes in his spontaneous, unforced verse.

But everywhere in Wesley, the real Wesley, we find another word, 'grace', almost its New Testament synonym, and for him it says the same evangelical thing:

> Not unto us, but thee, O Lord,
>   Glory to thee by given
> For every gracious thought and word
>   That brought us nearer heaven.   (*Works* iv, p 280)

('gracious' — of grace). Or another hymn:

> Mercy and grace are thine alone,
>   And power and wisdom too;
> Without the Spirit of thy Son
>   We nothing good can do.

'Mercy' and 'grace' and 'Spirit' all say the same — the absolute divine initiative, apart from which we are helpless:

> We cannot speak one useful word,
>   One holy thought conceive,
> Unless in answer to our Lord
>   Thyself the blessing give.   (*WH* 422-3)

This comes right back to the other hymn — 'every gracious thought'. Not only right words, but our right *thoughts* preceding were of grace. To stress the prevenience of grace is to approach the idea of election, and in these terms Wesley has the doctrine and only fears to name it. We can never get behind the first work of God in us, which is grace:

Thou great mysterious God unknown,
Whose love hath gently led me on,
Even from my infant days,

(that is, before any willed response from me)

Mine inmost soul expose to view,
And tell me if I ever knew
Thy justifying grace.

Whate'er obstructs thy pardoning love,
Or sin, or righteousness, remove,
Thy glory to display:

(that the work of righteousness be altogether God's)

Mine heart of unbelief convince,
And now absolve me from my sins,
And take them all away.   (*MHB* 376)

In all these hymns is the fundamental divine-human distinction:

Just and holy is thy name,
   I am all unrighteousness;
False and full of sin I am,
   Thou art full of truth and grace.

That is why salvation is altogether of God, his grace:

Let the utmost grace be given,
Save me quite from hell to heaven.   (*WH* 112)

That is, I have not gone some of the way to meet my Saviour, but he comes to
me at the very beginning of my need, and will see me right through. All is of
grace, so the first choice was God's choice of me.

Inseparable from grace in the New Testament, and defined by it (*Ro* 4:16;
Eph 1:8), is *faith*. Faith is *grace in us*, and only so our response *to grace*:

Faith in thy power thou seest I have,
   For thou this faith hast wrought,
Dead souls thou callest from their grave,
   And speakest worlds from nought

— faith being moral resurrection, of the creativity which makes worlds; it being 'God who quickeneth the dead, and calleth things that are not, as though they were' (*Ro* 4:17):

> Things that are not, as though they were,
>   Thou callest by their name;
> Present with thee the future [things] are,
>   With thee the great I AM

— which sounds very like predestination, whether Wesley knows it or not.

> The thing surpasses all my thought,
>   But faithful is my Lord;
> Through unbelief I stagger not,
>   For God hath spoke the word.
>
> Faith, mighty faith, the promise sees,
>   And looks to that alone,
> Laughs at impossibilities,
>   And cries, it shall be done!

— faith made possible only by the faithfulness of God. The hymn, headed *Romans* 4: 16 &c, is about Abraham's faith, and that is the New Testament norm for Christians.

A final verse, about faith's obedience, might seem different:

> Obedient faith that waits on thee
> Thou never wilt reprove ---.

But it is still Abraham's faith, that waits on God, and obeys: 'By faith Abraham --- obeyed.' This great word of *Hebrews* (11:8) must have been in mind, though the precise language is still *Romans* (1:5; 16:26) — 'obedience of faith'. It is the obedience that comes of faith, or is inherent in faith, so Wesley is right in making it adjectival to substantive faith — 'obedient faith'. But obedience it must be if we are to avoid the antinomian false track, of false faith. The doctrine is faith, but in practical terms we are to obey. This, for Wesley, finally means holiness, or perfect love, and he does not go outside the New Testament in saying so (*Gal* 1:16; 4:19; *I Jn* 4:12):

> --- But thou wilt form thy Son in me,
>   And perfect me in love.   (*WH* 350 — *HP* 693)

It is God who thus forms and perfects, the whole work being his work of grace. The hymn is faith, beginning to end, and the final faith-that-obeys tempers the Calvinism and saves it from itself. Say evangelical Arminianism, and you have said nothing different.

That is one of the very great hymns of evangelical religion — it is all prayer, the actual exercise of faith. A more theologically structured hymn, but still prayer, is about this same divine faith, with this first, that it had no antecedents in the believer before he believed, but its author is the Lord of faith and it is Spirit-breathed:

> Author of faith, eternal Word,
> Whose Spirit breathes the active flame —
> Faith, like its finisher and Lord,
> Today as yesterday the same.

Faith is gift, it is fire that has been lit:

> To thee our humble hearts aspire,
> And ask the gift unspeakable;
> Increase in us the kindled fire,
> In us the work of faith fulfil.

Faith is its own evidence, and owes nothing to human reason:

> The things unknown to feeble sense,
> Unseen by reason's glimmering ray,
> With strong commanding evidence
> Their heavenly origin display.

Faith has objective status as the other side of revelation:

> Faith lends its realizing light,
> The clouds disperse, the shadows fly,
> The invisible appears in sight,
> And God is seen by mortal eye. (*HP* 662)

Now all this precisely happened in the evangelical Revival, out of which Wesley wrote:

> See how great a flame aspires,
> Kindled by a spark of grace

— grace its absolute beginning, the first spark.

> O that all might catch the flame,
> All partake the glorious bliss!

— for all, but a flame that no man kindled.

> Now the word doth swiftly run,
> Now it wins its widening way

— the word of Jesus, with its own impetus and momentum as it runs and is glorified (*Ps* 147:15; *II Thess* 3:1 RV).

> More and more it spreads and grows,
> Ever mighty to prevail;
> Sin's strongholds it now o'erthrows,
> Shakes the trembling gates of hell

— the word against all opposition (*Ac* 12:24; 19:20; *II Co* 10:4; *Mt* 16:18 AV).

> Sons of God, your Saviour praise,
> He the door hath opened wide

— the door of faith, and he opens it (*Ac* 14:27).

> He hath given the word of gracc,
> Jesu's word is glorified

— 'the word of his grace' (*Ac* 14:3;20:32), and 'glorified' (again, *II Thess* 3:1).

> Jesus, mighty to redeem,
> He alone the work hath wrought;
> Worthy is the work of him,
> Him who spake a world from nought

— divine creation, as at the first : 'And God said' (*Ge* 1; *Ro* 4:17; *Heb* 1:2). The final picture (in a hymn packed with Bible images) is the weather, and God orders that — a perfect presentation of revival, which divinely happens:

> Saw ye not the cloud arise,
> Little as a human hand?
> Now it spreads along the skies,
> Hangs o'er all the thirsty land:
> Lo! the promise of a shower
> Drops already from above;
> But the Lord shall shortly pour
> All the Spirit of his love. (*HP* 781— *I K* 18:44f; *Joel* 2:28).

This characteristic hymn of the Revival has all the tones of Calvinism as to the absolute initiative of God, but the repeated 'all' of its opening verse has equally the tones of Arminian evangelism. This is essential Wesley, in saying both things together. It must not be thought that he halts between two opinions, writing now Arminian, now Calvinist hymns, according to mood and current persuasion. The *Hymns on God's Everlasting Love* are of purpose Arminian, but most of his other work is unpurposed Calvinist-Arminian. We instance three great evangelistic hymns, predictably Arminian, but not less Calvinist for that. And first:

> Spirit of Faith, come down,
> Reveal the things of God,
> And make to us the Godhead known,
> And witness with the blood:
> 'Tis thine the blood to apply,
> And give us eyes to see

(it is pure Calvinism — we see only as we are given eyes to see; until suddenly this)

> Who did for every sinner die
> Hath surely died for me

— his other argument in reverse:

> So wide it never passed by one,
> Or it had passed by me.   (*HP* 46)

.   .   .   .   .

> That all may hear the quickening sound,
> If I, even I, have mercy found!   (*HP* 185)

But quickly back to Calvinist bed-rock (*I Co* 12:3):

> No man can truly say
> That Jesus is the Lord,
> Unless thou take the veil away,
> And breathe the living word:
> Then, only then we feel
> Our interest in his blood,
> And cry with joy unspeakable
> Thou art my Lord, my God!

But on to this Arminian prayer:

> O that the world might know
> My dear atoning Lamb!
> Spirit of faith, descend, and show
> The virtue of his name:
> The grace which all may find,
> The saving power impart,
> And testify to all mankind,
> And speak in every heart.

84

(But see the Calvinism embedded in the Arminianism — only by the Spirit of Faith descending can all this be.) And the last verse, Calvinist and Arminian, about living faith that only the Holy Spirit can inspire (in-breathe), but that yet we have the responsibility of receiving:

> Inspire the living faith
> (Which whosoe'er receives
> The witness in himself he hath,
> And consciously believes),
> The faith that conquers all,
> And doth the mountain move,
> And saves whoe'er on Jesus call,
> And perfects them in love. (*HP* 325)

Another hymn that we can properly call Calvinist-Arminian goes back almost to the beginning of the Evangelical Revival, being 'FOR THE ANNIVERSARY DAY OF ONE'S CONVERSION' (Wesley's own after one year):

> O for a thousand tongues to sing
> My dear Redeemer's praise.

This is Calvinist if we think about it:

> He speaks; and, listening to his voice,
> New life the dead receive,
> The mournful broken hearts rejoice,
> The humble poor believe.
>
> Hear him, ye deaf; his praise, ye dumb,
> Your loosened tongues employ;
> Ye blind, behold your Saviour come,
> And leap, ye lame, for joy!

It is the poor in spirit who believe, so faith did not come of their own spirituality. And clearly, the dead cannot agree to be made alive, the deaf can hear by no faculty of their own hearing, and it was no use the blind deciding to see their Saviour come. Yet the hymn goes straight on, with no sense of contradiction, the sense rather of an inevitable logic of the gospel, to this challengingly Arminian conclusion:

> Look unto him, ye nations; own
> Your God, ye fallen race;
> Look, and be saved through faith alone,
> Be justified by grace.

See all your sins on Jesus laid;
  The Lamb of God was slain,
His soul was once an offering made
  For *every soul* of man.

This hymn, which held pride of place in Methodist hymn-books for two centuries, remains the manifesto of the Evangelical Revival, both wings of it.

Another great hymn of the Revival, almost twin to the foregoing (and equally well-served by the tune LYDIA), passes as quickly from the absolute divine action in redemption to a gospel for the world:

Jesus the prisoner's fetters breaks,
  And bruises Satan's head;
Power into strengthless souls it speaks,
  And life into the dead.

O that the world might taste and see
  The riches of his grace!
The arms of love which compass me
  Would all mankind embrace.   (*HP* 264)

Our thesis can be supported from both sides of the Calvinist-Arminian divide of the eighteenth century, for the Holy Spirit in Revival did not recognise the division. Despite ostensible difference, when it came to Bible preaching and practical evangelism the two sides met in the middle. Take this of Wesley's:

Come, sinners, to the gospel feast,
Let every soul be Jesu's guest,
You need not one be left behind,
For God hath bidden all mankind.

Sent by my Lord, on you I call,
The invitation is to all;
Come all the world; come, sinner, thou!
All things in Christ are ready now.

Come then, ye souls by sin opprest,
Ye restless wanderers after rest,
Ye poor, and maimed, and halt, and blind,
In Christ a hearty welcome find.

This is Arminian preaching, the open invitation. But it is not decisionism, but more and more manifestly the gospel of the love and power of God, his grace:

My message as from God receive,
Ye all may come to Christ, and live;
O let his love your hearts constrain,
Nor suffer him to die in vain.

His love is might to compel,
His conquering love consent to feel'
Yield to his love's resistless power,
And fight against your God no more.   (*WH* 2)

Put by this Whitefield's corresponding sermon on our Lord's parable (*Lk* 14: 22-24):

> Assure yourselves there is provision enough. For it is a great supper. In our Father's house there is bread enough and to spare ---. Neither can you complain of want of room, 'for yet there is room' ---. Come then, all ye halt, poor, maimed and blind sinners; take comfort, the Lord Jesus Christ has sent his servant to call you. It is now supper-time and a day of uncommon grace ---. What say you, my dear friends? I put the question to you once more, will you taste of Christ's supper, or will you not? You shall all be welcome ---. And O! that his love may excite us to come afresh to him ---. For, though we have been often feasted, yet our souls will starve, unless we renew our acts of faith, and throw ourselves, as lost, undone sinners, continually at the feet of Christ.

What do we make of these two very similar expositions, with the one invitation, 'come then'? 'Will you taste of Christ's supper, or will you not? You shall all be welcome' — 'his conquering love --- his love's resistless power'. Who is the Arminian, and who is the Calvinist? True, Whitefield has the saving words, 'O! that his love may excite us to come'; but they are not as strong as Wesley's 'His love is mighty to compel'. And from a viewpoint of strict Calvinism, will souls 'often feasted' ever possibly starve, and might the issue depend on our renewed acts of faith? No doubt the two would defend their respective positions, but it would be playing with words if these were words of this sermon and hymn, for in either case we could as easily prove the opposite. But they are not defending positions now, but preaching the Gospel (the hymn is preaching equally with the sermon), and as preachers together in the Revival they have one message and invitation from their Lord.

I might be challenged whether I am not trying to ride two horses at the same time — and more seriously, if I have rightly understood Wesley, whether he is not. Now if a single label be required, it has to be 'evangelical Arminian'. On the final issue of a limited atonement Wesley is Arminian, not Calvinist. But up to that point, it is the same message. He shares with Calvinists the fundamental doctrines of grace, faith, and the Holy Spirit. These are the Calvinist premiss, and he only does not make the Calvinist deduction from them. It is the Calvinist logic he rejects, not its substance. It is not sliding over differences to note the main area of agreement. The Wesleys were rightly scornful of the antinomian 'Calvinism' of their day, but their relation with Whitefield was different — though fellowship was at times strained, it never really broke.

———————

By 'the true Gospel' that 'touches the very edge of Calvinism' John Wesley meant evangelical Arminianism, and hymn after hymn of his brother's confirms this. There is an evangelical subtlety about them that gets right beneath the Calvinist-Arminian difference. Which side, for instance, may claim:

> Make me willing to be free,
> Restless to be saved by thee. (*WH* 166)

Wesley's most authentic writing is when he is not simply Arminian, and of course not simply Calvinist, but unconsciously both. When he gets beyond his polemic to his true spontaneity, when he is not defending a position but addressing himself believingly to his Lord, or proclaiming the Gospel to others, he is simply an evangelical Christian. He will not have Calvinism by the name, because he cannot accept a doctrine of limited grace-and-atonement, and also because he is appalled by current excesses; but he could not be more Calvinist in ascribing salvation, beginning with faith, altogether to the gracious will of God:

> Be it according to thy word! (*HP* 749)

———————

> And answer all thy righteous will. (*WH* 407)

———————

> And answer all they great design. (*MHB* 584)

———————

> Answer thy mercy's whole design. (*HP* 462)

Such, repeated endlessly, are Wesley's ultimates, his final explanation of how we come to be saved. Paramount always in these hymns is God's will for our salvation, and always his grace:

> Thy will is my salvation, Lord,
>   And let it now take place,
> And let me tremble at thy word
>   Of reconciling grace. (*WH* 298)

· · · · ·

He wills that I should holy be;
Who can withstand his will?
The counsel of his grace in me
He surely shall fulfil. (*HP* 731)

Salvation because God has willed to save me, holiness because he wills me holy (and who can withstand his will?) — it is all Wesley's very special, very Calvinist, brand of Arminianism; for always it is grace. It stops short of the rigour of 'the decrees', as the New Testament does; but in setting forth God's will for our salvation, which is finally our sanctification, it does in all but name set forth the New Testament doctrine of our election in grace.

So, acknowledging final mystery, our conclusion from these unique hymns is Calvinist and Arminian. It must be both, for there is Scripture support for the positive tenets of both. Our temptation as Calvinists or Arminians is to enjoy those scriptures that *we* find congenial, and turning a Nelson's eye on what we think we would be less happy with. Wesley-Arminian, we saw, does not wholly avoid this pitfall, but he does better than most of us. His religion is profounder than he knows, at cost of being less logical than he thinks. In all, and notwithstanding the Arminian war-cries of the two tracts, his hymns achieve an unrealised Calvinist-Arminian synthesis that is probably unique in Christian literature, and reflects more nearly than anything else I know the spirit of the Revival and of the New Testament.

11. THE SENSE OF GOD

Wesley's hymns at their frequent best are hymns of communion with God
— more than the contemplation of God, actual communion in the very hymns.
They have and convey a sense of God, and love for God:

> O love divine, how sweet thou art!
> When shall I find my willing heart
>   All taken up by thee?
> I thirst, and faint, and die to prove
> The greatness of redeeming love,
>   The love of Christ to me.
>
> Stronger his love than death or hell,
> Its riches are unsearchable;
>   The first-born sons of light
> Desire in vain its depth to see,
> They cannot reach the mystery,
>   The length, and breadth and height.
>
> God only knows the love of God,
> O that it now were shed abroad
>   In this poor stony heart!
> For love I sigh, for love I pine,
> This only portion, Lord, be mine,
>   Be mine this better part!
>
> O that I could for ever sit,
> With Mary, at the Master's feet!
>   Be this my happy choice!
> My only care, delight, and bliss,
> My joy, my heaven on earth be this,
>   To hear the Bridegroom's voice.   (*MHB* 434)

This is an amazing hymn, with white heat of emotion that is somehow right.
'For love I sigh, for love I pine' would ruin any other hymn, but here the love
does not get lost in itself. It is no mere sentiment. The hymn is about
redeeming love in its greatness, stronger than death or hell, known, in its
transcendent mystery, only to God who is very love:

> God only knows the love of God (*Eph* 3:18f)

Yet even the best such hymns have their obvious dangers, as Charles'
brother editorially recognised. That hymn he allowed, but only one reason
appears why he left out of his definitive hymn-book great hymns like *Jesu,*

lover and *Thou Shepherd of Israel.* The same trend of criticism is suggested by his elimination of 'dear-est' from lines he made into:

> My great Redeemer's throne.

> Thy nature, gracious Lord, impart.

> Thou loving, all-atoning Lamb.

But the criticism was not thorough-going. He retained:

> My dear Redeemer's praise.[1]

> Jesu, dear expected guest.

> His dear anointed one.

> The dear tokens of his passion.

> That dear disfigured face.

Barbarity alone could have tampered with these two last. But even Charles's weaker originals, 'Dear loving ... Lamb', 'dearest Lord', are in contexts quite unsentimental — the taking away of sin, a new heart, motifs evangelical and moral, not amorous (*HP* 185: 2; 536:5).

Nobody has better understood than Wesley the evangelical definition that the New Testament gives to *love.* Compare a classic of the Middle Ages, *Jesu, dulcis memoria,* with a characteristic hymn of the Evangelical Revival:

> O Jesus, thou the beauty of art
>   Of angel worlds above;
> Thy name is music to the heart,
>   Enchanting it with love.
>
> (from 'Jesu, the very thought of Thee', tr. E. Caswall).

— that is *eros* of a thousand love-poems, romantic or aesthetic love. Set it beside:

> Jesus, harmonious name,
>   It charms the hosts above;
> They evermore proclaim
>   And wonder at his love:
> 'Tis all their happiness to gaze,
> 'Tis heaven to see our Jesu's face.

His name the sinner hears,
    And is from sin set free;
'Tis music in his ears,
    'Tis life and victory:
New songs do now his lips employ,
And dances his glad heart for joy   (*WH* 33)

— that is *agape* of the New Testament, not love abstractly but the love of Jesus personally, evangelical love that is grace to sinners. *The name of Jesus, beauty, (harmony), angels (hosts), worlds above (heaven), music* (Wesley adds *dancing!), the heart, enchantment (charm)*, and of course *love* — it is the same field of vocabulary, but the hymns are not the same.   The difference is *love* as Wesley understands it evangelically from the New Testament.

In the Christian last analysis, love is what we predicate of God (*I Jn* 4:8):

Thy nature and the name is Love. (*HP* 434)

This love is the absolute initiative of the divine will:

He hath loved, he hath loved us, because he *would* love. (*MHB* 66)

For us, love is not attainment but experience:

The guiltless shame, the sweet distress,
The unutterable tenderness,
The genuine meek humility,
The wonder, why such love to me!

The o'erwhelming power of saving grace,
The sight that veils the seraph's face,
The speechless awe that dares not move.
And all the silent heaven of love. (*MHB* 325)

Christian love is Christ's love in Christians:

Write thy new name upon my heart,
    Thy new best name of LOVE. (*HP* 536).

Love to others is the constraint of his love:

O let me kiss thy bleeding feet,
    And bathe, and wash them with my tears,
The story of thy love repeat
    In every drooping sinner's ears,
That all may hear the quickening sound,
If[2] I, even I, have mercy found.

O let thy love my heart constrain,
   Thy love for every sinner free,
That every fallen soul of man
   May taste the grace that found out me,
That all mankind with me may prove
Thy sovereign everlasting love. (*HP* 185)

    .   .   .   .

There is another key-word in these contexts. The evangelical understanding of *love* is matched by an evangelical understanding of *holiness*, the
two being virtual synonyms in Wesley for the one work of grace:

Come, Saviour, come, and make me whole!
   Entirely all my sins remove;
To perfect health restore my soul,
   To perfect holiness and love. *(WH* 396)

Holiness is none other than the divine grace and love being perfected in us,
according to the will of God (*I.Thess* 4:3):

He wills that I should holy be:
   Who can withstand his will?
The counsel of his grace in me
   He surely shall fulfil. (*WH* 373)

    .   .   .   .

He wills that I should holy be;
   That holiness I long to feel,
That full divine conformity
   To all my Saviour's righteous will:
See, Lord, the travail of thy soul
   Accomplished in the change of mine,
And plunge me, every whit made whole,
   In all the depths of love divine. (*WH* 396)

There is a God-honouringness in this. Holiness, being love, is of God, indeed
is his love and holiness, the only reason why we should be holy and the only
way we can. It is 'the travail of his soul accomplished in the change of mine'
— the concept is thoroughly evangelical. It is strictly an attribute of God,
ours only as we share the divine nature and holiness:

Let me of thy life partake,
   Thy own holiness impart. (*MHB* 876; *II Pe* 1:4; *Heb* 12:10)

It is here that Wesley among hymn-writers has a possibly unequalled sense of the immanence and at the same time the transcendence of God — transcendent God immanent. He is my life, but he is always God:

> Abba, Father! hear thy child
> Late in Jesus reconciled;
> Hear, and all the graces shower,
> All the joy and peace and power,
> All my Saviour asks above,
> All the life and heaven of love.
>
> Heavenly Adam, life divine,
> Change my nature into thine;
> Move and spread throughout my soul,
> Actuate and fill the whole;
> Be it I no longer now
> Living in the flesh, but thou.
>
> Holy Ghost, no more delay,
> Come, and in thy temple stay;
> Now thy inward witness bear,
> Strong, and permanent and clear;
> Spring of life, thyself impart,
> Rise eternal in my heart. (*MHB* 568)

The profound basis of this holiness hymn is the Christian doctrine of God, Father, Son, and Holy Spirit. And it is the underlying Trinitarian doctrine that keeps even bolder words 'sane and reverent and orthodox'[3]:

> When shall I see the welcome hour,
>   That plants my God in me,
> Spirit of health and life and power
>   And perfect liberty!
>
> Jesu, thy all-victorious love
>   Shed in my heart abroad!
> Then shall my feet no longer rove,
>   Rooted and fixed in God. (*WH* 351)

Such audacity might give us pause, and ought to. But it has the authority of the New Testament — texts like *John* 15:5; *Galatians* 1:16; 2:20; 4:19; *Ephesians* 3:17; *Colossians* 1:27; *I John* 4:13. In these, God is the sole sanctifier, for the life of holiness is never other than his life in our lives.

Thus far we must agree, even if we have not yet got that far. What is more problematical is the perfectionism of some of Wesley's early hymns. Indeed their ground is evangelical, with logic that at the time must have seemed unanswerable:

> If nothing is too hard for thee,
> All things are possible to me.

The sinless life is possible because nothing is *impossible* to God. It is the privilege of God's children:

> All things are possible to God,
>   To Christ the power of God in man,
> To me, when I am all renewed,
>   When I in Christ am born again,
> And witness, from all sin set free,
> All things are possible to me. *(HP 723)*

But this is not as confident as it sounds, for Charles knows his own heart, that 'all' is not yet. That can only mean he is not yet a child of God, and he is forced to look to a time when in Christ he is 'born again'. John rightly softened this into 'formed again' (small as the difference might be), for if Charles meant he was doubting his present state of regeneracy, then Charles was surely wrong. His logical impasse came because his premiss was wrong: that to be a child of God is to be altogether holy. Oddly, he seems more confident of entire sanctification as a near prospect than of justification now. He has rather confused the two, in speaking of being 'born again' to a sinless life.

This regenerative view of holiness has for Wesley the further consequence that sanctification is event rather than process:

> O Jesus, at thy feet we wait
>   Till thou shalt bid us rise,
> Restored to our unsinning state,
>   To love's sweet paradise. *(WH 378)*

How literally do we take this? It seems to be saying that when we rise to our feet, we are perfect in love — or certainly that this can and does happen. Similarly:

> What is our calling's glorious hope
>   But inward holiness?
> For this to Jesus I look up,
>   I calmly wait for this.

The picture is of my sitting, or kneeling, waiting for holiness *to happen,* as following lines confirm:

> I wait, till he shall touch me clean.

> Surely it shall on me take place . *(HP 749)*

95

The idea is *instant sanctification*, though the instant may not be quite yet. In principle, there must be a moment when it happens. Thus, *Lord I believe a rest remains* — the sabbath-rest for the people of God (*Heb* 4:9, anticipating the 1880 Revisers):

> To me the rest of faith impart,
> The sabbath of thy love.

The 'rest' is love perfected,

> Where doubt, and fear, and pain expire,[4]
> Cast out by perfect love.   (*I Jn* 4:18)

And it can happen *now,* by faith:

> O that I now the rest might know,
> Believe , and enter in!
> Now, Saviour, now the power bestow,
> And let me cease from sin. (*HP* 736)

John, in his *Plain Account of Christian Perfection,* cites this hymn as evidence of the Methodist holiness teaching, picking out this word 'now' — full salvation, by faith, in an instant, that may be *now*.   And next in his hymnbook is another with same word in same context of the promised land:

> O glorious hope of perfect love!
> It lifts me up to things above,
>   It bears on eagles' wings:
> It gives my ravished soul a taste,
> And makes me for some moments feast
>   With Jesu's priests and kings.
>
> Rejoicing now in earnest hope,
> I stand, and from the mountain top
>   See all the land below ...
>
> O that I might at once go up,
> No more on this side Jordan stop,
>   But now the land possess! ...
>
> Now, O my Joshua, bring me in!
> Cast out my foes; the inbred sin,
>   The carnal mind remove:
> The purchase of thy death divide,
> And O! with all the sanctified
>   Give me a lot of love.   (*WH* 392; *Josh* 14:2)

His gospel inheritance, which is love, might be realised *at once, now.*

So what do we make of these hymns, and the hope of love, or holiness, in them? At times and in one aspect they seem self-absorbed, with interest more in a psychological state of 'love' than at all love recognisable in New Testament terms; and the insistent demanding 'now' strengthens this impression. Yet it is very partially true. Love's inheritance is to love God, and that is not self-absorbed. There is a paradox here, almost inevitable in hymns so personal. The hymns are intimately about self, but their end is God, and loving God. So *Lord I believe,* which continues:

> I would be thine, thou know'st I would,
>   And have thee all my own;
> Thee, O my all-sufficient good,
>   I want,[5] and thee alone.
>
> Thy name to me, thy nature grant,
>   This, only this be given;
> Nothing beside my God I want,[5]
>   Nothing in earth or heaven.   (*MIIB* 563 — *HP* 736)

These hymns are about that holiness without which no man shall see the Lord. They are God-absorbed. A parallel hymn[6] makes the same progression from the aspiration after holiness to communion with God, and it is where the hymn gets to that finally matters. We might demur at the three-fold 'I' of:

> I even I, shall see his face,
>   I shall be holy here!

(Compare the three-fold 'now' of the other hymn). But the end is beautiful:

> My earth thou water'st from on high,
>   But make it all a pool!
> Spring up, O well, I ever cry,
>   Spring up within my soul!
>
> Come, O my God, thyself reveal,
>   Fill all his mighty void!
> Thou only canst my spirit fill:
>   Come, O my God, my God!
>
> Fulfil, Fulfil my large desires,
>   Large as infinity!
> Give, give me all my soul requires,
>   All, all that is in thee!   (*WH* 393)

Our hesitation over some of this language might well be our own problem — both that Wesley is a poet and we (most of us) are not poets, and that we may not have the spiritual sensitivity, the sense of God, that he has. Such verses, and these hymns overall, so much about ourselves and so much more about God, are not a contradiction but are the true orthodoxy. *Galatians* 2:20 *is* about self — I do live, though paradoxically it is no longer I but Christ living in me. The annihilation of self, rather than its redemption, is Buddhist, not Christian. We keep the paradox, and the end word is God.

．　．　．　．　．

But these are a category of hymn we will be wise to use sparingly. Even with instant sanctification ironed out of them, indeed all the more then, we are on high and holy ground, and that is why we cannot stay long in so rarefied an atmosphere. Thankfully we need not, for Wesley has other holiness hymns that start nearer where we are:

> O for an heart to praise my God,
> An heart from sin set free,
> An heart that always feels thy blood
> So freely spilt for me!

— *always*. This hymn goes on to picture the new heart — his dear Redeemer's throne; believing, true and clean; full of love divine. But he will never be in a position of not needing the grace of Christ, his blood. Not, of course, that any hymn of Wesley's ever contemplated he might! But it is different from the triumphalist 'I shall be holy here!'

In another great hymn, mystical and dying and rising with Christ is only consequent upon *his saving* cross:

> Thou hast undertook for me,
> For me to death wast sold;
> Wisdom in a mystery
> Of bleeding love unfold:
> Teach the lesson of thy cross,
> Let me die with thee to reign,
> All things let me count but loss
> So I may thee regain.

The way of holiness has to be the way of penitence:

> Show me, as my soul can bear,
> The depth of inbred sin;
> All the unbelief declare,
> The pride that lurks within:
> Take me, whom thyself hast bought,
> Bring into captivity
> Every high aspiring thought
> That would not stoop to thee.

Frankly, that is a note we missed from some of the others. Is there just the danger that holiness itself can be a high aspiring thought, way up on cloud nine? Here is the infinite divine patience, with sin exposed only gradually as the soul can bear. Sanctification is for the slow of heart, and in God's good time:

> Lord, my time is in thy hand,
>   My soul to thee convert;
> Thou canst make me understand,
>   Though I am slow of heart.

It could be significant that the actual aspiring words, 'holy', 'holiness', are nowhere in the hymn. Wesley knows their right use, but this hymn the more impresses for being without them. Yet he reaches the same uttermost conclusion:

> Thine, in whom I live and move,
>   Thine the work, the praise is thine;
> Thou art wisdom, power, and love,
>   And all thou art is mine. (*HP* 540)

He has more low-key hymns like these two, and some, as well as being modest in their choice of words, have a healthy regard for practicalities:

> If so poor a worm as I
>   May to thy great glory live,
> All my actions sanctify,
>   All my words and thoughts receive;
> Claim me, for thy service claim,
> All I have and all I am.

(The despised hymnic worm may have been a corrective to some of the higher flights!)

> Take my soul and body's powers,
>   Take my memory, mind, and will,
> All my goods and all my hours,
>   All I know, and all I feel,
> All I think, and speak, and do;
> Take my heart — but make it new. (*HP* 791)

. . . . .

> Me if thy grace vouchsafe to use,
>   Meanest of all thy creatures, me,
> The deed, the time, the manner choose;
>   Let all my fruit be found of thee:
> Let all my works in thee be wrought,
> By thee to full perfection brought.

(Not 'Now, Saviour, now' but 'The deed, the time, the manner choose')

> My every weak, though good, design,
>   O'errule or change, as seems thee meet;
> Jesus, let all my work be thine!
>   Thy work, O Lord, is all-complete,
> And pleasing in thy Father's sight;
> Thou only hast done all things right. (*HP* 788)

These are noticeably different from his more perfectionist hymns cited earlier, but they no less look towards perfection. And they all date together, in the 1740s. The difference was never absolute, for all are evangelically based — Wesley was always clear about holiness the work of God in a believer. But there is a more evident humility about these last-cited, and it was this that prevailed in his important 1762 *Short Hymns on Select Passages of the Holy Scriptures*. His prayer is still for holiness, but this means God's law written on his heart:

> That blessed law of thine,
>   Jesus, to me impart;
> The Spirit's law of life divine
>   O write it on my heart.
>
> Implant it deep within,
>   Whence it may ne'er remove,
> The law of liberty from sin,
>   The perfect law of love. (*MHB* 547)

It is the law, or principle, of holiness that is perfect, and Wesley is not exactly looking at himself as holy. And these hymns have a practicality that grounds them firmly in reality:

> I want the witness, Lord,
>   That all I do is right,
> According to thy will and word,
>   Well-pleasing in thy sight. (*HP* 293)

This too is practical:

> Jesus, confirm my heart's desire
>   To work, and speak, and think for thee;
> Still let me guard the holy fire,
>   And still stir up thy gift in me:
> Ready for all thy perfect will,
>   My acts of faith and love repeat,
> Till death thy endless mercies seal
>   And make my sacrifice complete.

The holy fire is the flame of love, that makes me ready for God's perfect will; and my acts of faith and love are then my spiritual sacrifice. This is bold, yet humble, for not till death is the sacrifice complete.

Meantime, through life, the other side of all this activity is the passivity of penitence and submission. (These are all the *Short Hymns):*

> Lord, that I may learn of thee,
> Give me true simplicity;
> Wean my soul, and keep it low,
> Willing thee alone to know.
>
> Let me cast myself aside,
> All that feeds my knowing pride,
> Not to man but God submit,
> Lay my reasonings at thy feet.
>
> Of my boasted wisdom spoiled,
> Docile, helpless as a child,
> Only seeing in thy light,
> Only walking in thy might.
>
> Then infuse the teaching grace,
> Spirit of truth and righteousness;
> Knowledge, love divine impart,
> Life eternal to my heart. (*HP* 737)

Perhaps the most important words here, out of many important words, are 'love divine' — his earlier prayer, for

> An heart in every thought renewed,
> And full of love divine.

That hymn was beautifully humble in spirit, and this now presses further the actualities of *being humbled* — the weaning of the soul, the casting aside of self, the spoiling of natural wisdom, the infusing of grace.

In a word, these hymns are about the sanctification *process*, and the idea now is progressive holiness, or love being perfected. Charles has significantly modified his brother's and his own former view, has grown decisively away from the notion of instant holiness, even by faith, and still more from any thought of claiming to have it, even to God's glory. He now sees personal holiness only in terms of profound paradox:

> Ye that do your Master's will,
> Meek in heart, be meeker still;
> Righteous, still yourselves confess
> Seekers after righteousness;
> Gracious souls, in grace abound,
> Seek the Lord whom ye have found.

Bridges' recast of the second couplet is sensitively done, keeping the spirit of it:

> Day by day your sins confess,
> Ye that walk in righteousness.

Perhaps we should accept this, but there was nothing wrong with what Wesley wrote. It is his final paradox of Christian experience — have, yet seeking still:

> Sing, ye happy souls that press
> Toward the height of holiness;
> All his promises receive,
> All the grace he hath to give;
> Follow on, nor slack your pace,
> Till ye see his glorious face. (*MHB* 628[7])

It is good the hymn is in the plural, reminding us that holiness is no private possession or personal accomplishment. But a similar and equally beautiful short hymn is in purely personal terms:

> Jesus, the First and Last,
> On thee my soul is cast;
> Thou didst thy work begin
> By blotting out my sin;
> Thou wilt the root remove,
> And perfect me in love.
>
> But when the work is done,
> The work is but begun;
> Partaker of thy grace,
> I long to see thy face;
> The first I prove below,
> The last I die to know. (*HP* 735)

Thus does Charles in devotional verse succeed in saying what John in prose argument never quite convincingly worked out. Holiness is not some graduation in religion, that distinguishes certain Christians. Rather, it is ongoing as we go on with Christ. Consummation is not yet — the beatific vision I only die to know. But his grace I prove below. I really am in a state of grace, while not yet perfected. 'Not that I have already obtained, or am already made perfect: but I press on' — as the first of the two hymns says (*Phil* 3:12, again *RV*). Perfection is a real, and certain, prospect, but it is a process:

102

What now is my object and aim?
    What now is my hope and desire?
To follow the heavenly Lamb,
    And after his image aspire:
My hope is all centred in thee,
    I trust to recover thy love,
On earth thy salvation to see,
    And then to enjoy it above.   (*WH* 360; *Ps* 39:8, *BCP*)

What does he mean by 'seeing' God's salvation? and what is salvation in these terms? It clearly is full salvation, and he goes on to say that its enjoyment is 'above'. The suggestion is of a Pisgah experience here on earth, preview only of our final estate of blessedness. He had used that precise image in an earlier hymn (*WH* 393, quoted p 97):

The promised land from Pisgah's top
    I now exult to see;
My hope is full (O blessed hope!)
    Of immortality.

These beautiful lines, surpassed only by Watts's supreme poetry of the scene, *There is a land of pure delight,* have something of the same facility in use of a proper noun. Our one criticism is that he does not sustain the image, as Watts did through the six verses of his hymn, but succeeding verses speak rather of 'near approach' and 'this glad day'. But now, two decades later, it is again 'object and aim', 'hope and desire', not the old instant sanctification. So too an exposition of *Psalm* 81:10 with *Ephesians* 3:18f — the ultimate aspiration, to be filled with the fulness of God; but faith's capacity must be stretched ever wider to receive it:

Give me that enlarged desire,
    And open, Lord, my soul,
Thy own fulness to require,
    And comprehend the whole:
Stretch my faith's capacity
    Wider and yet wider still;
Then, with all that is in thee
    My soul forever fill! (*WH* 361)

What these hymns, even the rather less satisfactory among them, are saying, is that holiness is of God, actually his grace and love in us. When most ours, it is least ours:

The purest saint that lives below
    Doth his own sanctity disclaim;
The wisest owns, I nothing know,
    The holiest cries, I nothing am! (*Works* ix, p 238; *Job* 9:20)

103

No holy man ever congratulated himself on his holiness:

> That voice which speaks Jehovah near,
> That still small voice I long to hear;
> O might it now the Lord proclaim,
> And fill my soul with holy shame:
> Ashamed I must for ever be,
> Afraid the God of love to see,
> If saints and prophets hide their face
> And angels tremble while they gaze.
> (WH 413; IK 19:12f; cp HP 540: 1,2)

Personal holiness is never as great a matter as holy God, and he is far from holy who fails to recognise this:

> Holy as thee,[8] O Lord, is none,
> Thy holiness is all thine own;
> A drop of that unbounded sea
> Is ours, a drop derived from thee;
> And when thy purity we share,
> Thine only glory we declare,
> And humbled into nothing, own
> Holy and pure is God alone. (WH 238; I Sa 2:2)

Which comes surprisingly near to noble lines that nobody would associate with Wesley but that have the same source in Scripture:

> Holy, holy, holy! though the darkness hide thee,
>   Though the eye of sinful man thy glory may not see;
> Only thou art holy, there is none beside thee,
>   Perfect in power, in love, and purity. (HP 7)

Undergirding experimental holiness, which could separate Heber from Charles Wesley (though more from John), is the doctrine of holy God, fundamental, and fundamentally the same, for both.

All those were the *Short Hymns*, with their more complete humility before the holiness of God. They represent Wesley's mature spirituality, though some of his earlier hymns anticipate this. *O for an heart to praise my God* and *Open, Lord, my inward ear* come twenty years before,[9] and with them his (and the world's?) greatest holiness hymn of all:

> God of all power, and truth, and grace,
>   Which shall from age to age endure,
> Whose word, when heaven and earth shall pass,
>   Remains, and stands for ever sure.

This has begun right away from self, with the very being and word of God. Then at once the only true motivation of a holy life:

> That I thy mercy may proclaim,
>   That all mankind thy truth may see,

and the only way of it:

> Hallow thy great and glorious name,
>   And perfect holiness in me.

Holiness is God's hallowing of his own name in his people, even as our Lord taught us to pray. The precise expression 'perfecting holiness' is Paul's at *II Corinthians* 7:1, being the exhortation to do just that. But here in Wesley it is not exhortation but prayer, and he has more in mind another Pauline text, *Philippians* 1:6: 'He which began a good work in you will perfect it (yet again *RV*) 'until the day of Jesus Christ'. Only so can we perfect holiness in the fear of God — as he perfects holiness in us. A following verse goes back to the Philippians text (confirming he has it in mind), but now in its *AV* rendering (for his Greek and English New Testaments were together in his mind):

> Perform the work thou hast begun...

All follows from this — it is the good work of God:

> Thy sanctifying Spirit pour...

> Purge me from every sinful blot...

> Give me a new, a perfect heart ...

> Cause me to walk in Christ my way...

And the end of the Christian walk is Canaan and the Sabbath-rest for the people of God:

> O that I now, from sin released,
>   Thy word might to the utmost prove,
> Enter into the promised rest,
>   The Canaan of thy perfect love.

Again the word favoured by these early holiness hymns of Charles's 'now'. But they are not all alike. 'O that I now ... might' is different in tone from the peremptory 'Now, Saviour, now' of the other hymn. John predictably read 'may' for 'might', making it less diffident. But is not the measure of diffidence right? Wesley is praying for love's perfection, yet never without the penitence he will always in this life feel before holy God:

Thy faithful mercies let me find
In which thou causest me to trust;
Give me the meek and lowly mind,
And lay my spirit in the dust.

Show me how foul my heart hath been,
When all renewed by grace I am;
When thou hast emptied me of sin,
Show me the fulness of my shame.

And on to the hymn's end, and its sum, which is not a saint but Christ:

Now let me gain perfection's height,
Now let me into nothing fall

('now' again, repeated, but see what he expects now!)

Be less than nothing in thy sight,
And feel that Christ is all in all.   (*HP* 726)[10]

That is holiness — Christ all in all.[10]

NOTES

1. After hesitation. Ms Colman 21 in John's hand, and 1778 draft, have 'great' and this was the preferred reading from 1798 onwards.
2. 'If indeed' — not doubt, but wonder.
3. Bernard Manning's words, about another Wesley hymn. (See second paper, *What We Have Felt,* note 15).
4. John made it 'fear, and sin, and grief' (which *HP* still has) — bringing in sinless perfection; and also avoiding the idea of freedom necessarily from pain.
5. See first paper, *The Handmaid of Piety,* note 18.
6. The two hymns being respective finales of *Hymns and Sacred Poems,* 1740 and 1742.
7. *Works* x, p 104 (*Zeph* 2:3) p 37 (*Jer* 31:12). The brilliant editing which brought these together, with Bridges's couplet, we owe to *MHB.*
8. Change to 'thou' was introduced, likely by another hand, in ed 7 of John's *Collection* 1791.
9. *Hymns and Sacred Poems* 1742.
10. *Works,* ii, p 319. Appended in full to John's sermon on CHRISTIAN PERFECTION.

12. THE GOSPEL CHURCH

Charles Wesley is principally recognised for his hymns of personal faith and devotion. *Jesu, lover of my soul, Open, Lord, my inward ear, O love divine, how sweet thou art!* are a random few of his finest — and of course *Wrestling Jacob*. But they are not a separate category of private, non-church hymn. Though each is in the first-person-singular throughout, they were from the first sung by the fellowship, along with others of his that say the same things in the plural of shared experience. Thus:

> O that in me the sacred fire
>   Might now begin to glow,
> Burn up the dross of base desire
>   And make the mountains flow!
>
> O that it now from heaven might fall
>   And all my sins consume!
> Come, Holy Ghost, for thee I call,
>   Spirit of burning, come!
>
> Refining fire, go through my heart,
>   Illuminate my soul;
> Scatter thy life through every part
>   And sanctify the whole   (*HP* 740)

— put this in the plural, and it is the same:

> Jesu, attend! thyself reveal!
>   Are we not met in thy great name?
> Thee in the midst we wait to feel,
>   We wait to catch the spreading flame.
>
> Thou God that answerest by fire,
>   The Spirit of burning now impart,
> And let the flames of pure desire
>   Rise from the altar of our heart.   (*MHB* 710)

There is really no difference in the sort of hymn — both are hymns of experience, about when the Spirit comes, and praying for this in the same figure of *fire*. The expression 'our heart' is characteristic Wesley — it means each one of our hearts, and our hearts as one. Compare:

> Preach his gospel to our heart.   (*HP* 298)

> And tune thy people's heart.   (*HP* 761)

With Wesley, one Christian's experience and the experience of Christians together are in essence the same, and he can pass naturally from one to the other in the space of two lines:

> How happy the man whose heart is set free,
> The people that can be joyful in thee. (*HP* 569)

> Pronounce the glad word and bid us be free;
> Ah! hast thou not, Lord, a blessing for me?   (*MHB* 747)

It is the same either way — of a Christian, or Christians:

> Saviour, I thank thee for the grace,
>   The gift unspeakable,
> And wait with arms of faith to embrace
> And all thy love to feel. (*HP* 733)

. . . . .

> The gift which he on one bestows
>   We all delight to prove;
> The grace through every vessel flows
>   In purest streams of love   (*HP* 753)

— it is the same vocabulary of *grace, gift, love*. Or place together these very similar verses (form and content) of different hymns:

> Yet onward I haste
>   To the heavenly feast;
> That, that is the fulness, but this is the taste:
>   And this I shall prove
>   Till with joy I remove
> To the heaven of heavens of Jesus's love. (*HP* 563)

. . . . .

> Nay, and when we remove
>   To the mansions above,
> Our heaven shall still be to sing of thy love:
>   We all shall commend
>   The love of our friend,
> For ever beginning what never shall end. (*MHB* 66)

These are pilgrim hymns — the pilgrim, but now the pilgrim Church. True, the first says nothing about other pilgrims — but a feast is a social event!

No Wesley hymns are more characteristic than these of pilgrimage. Most are of the pilgrim band — hymns of corporate experience:

108

Through thee, who all our sins hast borne,
   Freely and graciously forgiven,
With songs to Sion we return,
   Contending for our native heaven:
That palace of our glorious king,
We find it nearer while we sing. (*HP* 819)

. . . . .

Sing, ye happy souls that press
Toward the height of holiness;
All his promises receive,
All the grace he hath to give;
Follow on, nor slack your pace
Till ye see his glorious face. (*MHB* 628)

. . . . .

Our Brother, Saviour, Head,
   Our all in all is he;
And in his steps who tread
   We soon his face shall see,
Shall see him with our glorious friends,
And then in heaven our journey ends. (*MHB* 606)

. . . . .

Our strength, thy grace; our rule, thy word;
Our end, the glory of the Lord. (*HP* 62)

We may add some that begin with the Christian pilgrim but end with the Church in heaven:

How happy every child of grace
   Who knows his sins forgiven!
This earth, he cries, is not my place,
   I seek my place in heaven:
A country far from mortal sight,
   Yet O! by faith I see
The land of rest, the saints' delight,
   The heaven prepared for me.

But this is no private little heaven, prepared for just Charles! It is the saints' delight — and *our* hope:

O what a blessed hope is ours!
　　While here on earth we stay,
We more than taste the heavenly powers
　　And antedate that day:
We feel the resurrection near,
　　Our life in Christ concealed,
And with his glorious presence here
　　Our earthen vessels filled.　　(*MHB* 627)

(Note plural pronoun or possessive in six out of eight lines).　Again,

No foot of land do I possess,
No cottage in this wilderness;
　　A poor wayfaring man,
I lodge awhile in tents below,
Or gladly wander to and fro
　　Till I my Canaan gain.

This looks altogether too personal, even biographical, for a Church hymn, though it is not literally about Wesley's worldly estate (he didn't actually live in tents!), but is about the Christian in the world (*Acts* 7:5), and finally the perseverance of the saints.　When Wesley (in anticipation) reaches home, his elder brothers are there to welcome him in:

There is my house and portion fair,
My treasure and my heart is there,
　　And my abiding home:
　For me my elder brethren stay,
And angels beckon me away,
　　And Jesus bids me come. (*WH* 66)

One fine hymn ending with the Church in heaven is specially instructive here — *Shepherd divine*.　Its first half is the fellowship at prayer:

The Spirit of interceding grace
　　Give us in faith to claim,
To wrestle till we see thy face
And know thy hidden name.

Transition now to the singular of personal experience, maintained to the end of the hymn:

Till thou the perfect love impart,
　　Till thou thyself bestow,
Be this the cry of every heart,
　　I will not let thee go!

110

But note — 'every heart'. This is certainly Wesley's own heart-cry, but every one in the fellowship cries:

> Then let me on the mountain-top
> Behold thy open face. (*HP* 558)

The hymn is about the Church, even every member of it. (*MHB* had it in the section, *The Church in Prayer,)*

In fact, Wesley's Church hymns are among his hymns of personal experience, being experience together in the Body of Christ. This common experience of Christ found distinctive expression in the characteristic Methodist institutions of class-meeting and love-feast, and Wesley's fellowship hymns were specifically for these. This for the love-feast:

> God his blessings shall dispense,
> God shall crown his ordinance,
> Here is his appointed ways
> Nourish us with social grace. (*HP* 756)

'Social grace' is not when the Church takes time off from being religious, but when the fellowship meets in the name of Jesus:

> We meet the grace to take
> Which thou hast freely given. (*HP* 760)

> .   .   .   .   .

> The grace through every vessel flows,
> In purest streams of love. (*HP* 753)

> .   .   .   .   .

> ...Use the grace on each bestowed ,
> Tempered by the art of God. (*HP* 764)

This corporateness of personal grace is seen most of all in Wesley's Communion hymns. They are not less Church hymns when in the singular:

> Because thou hast said,
> 'Do this for my sake',
> The mystical bread
> I gladly partake. (*HP* 598)

Hymns and Psalms, whose is the credit for introducing this little gem, puts it in the plural — not altering its character, for we sing it together anyway. It is exactly the same when in the plural to begin with:

Jesu, we thus obey
Thy last and kindest word;
Here in thine own appointed way
We come to meet our Lord. (*HP* 614)

It is individual believers who come, and thy constitute the Israel of God:

See where our great High-priest
Before the Lord appears,
And on his loving breast
The tribes of Israel bears,
Never without his people seen,
The Head of all believing men. (*HP* 622)

The holy supper is the supreme fellowship meal, of which each one partakes:

Who thy mysterious supper share,
Here at thy table fed,
Many, and yet but one we are,
One undivided bread.

One with the living bread divine
Which now by faith we eat,
Our hearts and minds and spirits join,
And all in Jesus meet. (*HP* 609)

.   .   .   .   .

Effectual let the tokens prove,
And made, by heavenly art,
Fit channels to convey thy love
To every faithful heart. (*HP* 602)

This same love, or grace, of Christ, that we together claim, is for every
member of Christ:

Victim divine, thy grace we claim,
While thus thy precious death we show.

To every faithful soul appear,
And show thy real presence here. (*HP* 629)

All this entails a thoroughly evangelical doctrine of the Church, and not
only is it not the Church which overlooks the Gospel, it is not the Gospel
which overlooks the Church. This is 'the Gospel Church' (*HP* 438),

112

The Church of pardoned sinners
 Exulting in their Saviour (*HP* 440)

— the gathered Church, that is, 'of practical believers' (*HP* 440). Its relation
then to the institutional Church was not the problem for Charles that it might
be for some others:

The Church of Christ *and England* is but one! (*Rep. Verse* 257)

That seems rather much to say, but what he feared was sectarianism, and
anyway his passionate loyalty to the episcopal and national Church was never
expendable. Yet it is fair to say that his profoundest understanding of the
Church, as in his truest Church hymns, is evangelical from the New Testament
— Christ's mystic Body, in which every member feels its share.

13. TO SERVE THE PRESENT AGE

Wesley's hymns are not only about a Christian's inner life, or even life in the Body of Christ. They are about both these, but have a third dimension — the life of the world:

> Jesu's love the nations fires,
>   Sets the kingdoms on a blaze.

Not that hymns like this exactly anticipate the radical hymns of today, with their first concern for a Christian social order. Wesley's remain hymns of personal religion — about Christians and their influence then in the world:

> O that all might catch the flame,
>   All partake the glorious bliss. (*HP* 781)

Or another hymn of what we might call Wesley's personalised world-view (the world as people):

> O wouldst thou again be made known,
>   Again in thy Spirit descend,
> And set up in each of thine own
>   A kingdom that never shall end:
> Thou only art able to bless,
>   And make the glad nations obey,
> And bid the dire enmity cease,
>   And bow the whole world to thy sway. (*HP* 400)

This is more than pietistic, for it does look to a renewed earth, but it is the evangelical concept of personal renewal as the way of the kingdom — 'in each of thine own'.

We must look elsewhere than to Wesley for hymns directly about the world we live in, and our Christian mission to it. Wesley's *more radical* approach is *Christians*, and a Christian presence in the world. He was a man of his times, and conservative at that, judging from his satirical verses on contemporary issues and events.[1] These were dated before their ink dried, but his hymns of Christian vocation are valid today. 'To serve the present age' is always valid. And for him, that begins with the fundamental validity of Christian character:

> That wisdom, Lord, on us bestow,
>   From every evil to depart,
> To stop the mouth of every foe,
>   While, upright both in mind and heart,
> The proofs of godly fear we give,
> And shew them how the Christians live. (*WH* 310)

.   .   .   .   .

114

Thus may I show thy Spirit within,
    Which purges me from every stain;
Unspotted from the world and sin,
    My faith's integrity maintain,
The truth of my religion prove
    By perfect purity and love. (*HP* 318)

This is what makes impact on the world, as in the New Testament:

Jesus, let all thy lovers shine
    Illustrious as the sun,
And bright with borrowed rays divine
    Their glorious circuit run.

Beyond the reach of mortals, spread
    Their light where'er they go,
And heavenly influences shed
    On all the world below.

As the bright Sun of Righteousness
    Their healing wings display,
And let their lustre still increase
    Unto the perfect day. (*MHB* 603)

. . . . .

Us who climb thy holy hill
    A general blessing make;
Let the world our influence feel,
    Our gospel-grace partake. (*WH* 412)

One verifiable aspect of Christian character is application to daily work in the sight of God:

Forth in thy name, O Lord, I go,
    My daily labour to pursue,
Thee, only thee, resolved to know,
    In all I think or speak or do.

Thee may I set at my right hand,
    Whose eyes my inmost substance see,
And labour on at thy command
    And offer all my works to thee. (*HP* 381)

. . . . .

End of my every action thou,
   Thyself in all I see;
Accept my hallowed labour now,
   I do it unto thee.

Whate'er the Father views as thine
   He views with gracious eyes;
Jesus, this mean oblation join
   To thy great sacrifice. (*WH* 312)

                .   .   .   .   .

Their earthly task who fail to do
Neglect their heavenly business too ...
Asunder put what God hath joined,
A diligent and pious mind.

Happy we live, when God doth fill
Our hands with work, our hearts with zeal...
And like the blessed spirits above,
The more we serve, the more we love.   (*Works* xiii, p 17)

We recognise in these hymns a modern theme — the sanctity of work and its moral character as service. But they have not been bettered in our day.

Altogether, Wesley has a healthy regard for the normalities — daily work, and along with that, the marriage relationship. With one part-exception, his marriage hymns have never been recognised for what they are. Charles himself scarcely did, though he wrote them for his bride, Sarah Gwynne, or with her in mind. He published them later in the year of their marriage, but grouped with hymns for the fellowship like *Jesus, we look to Thee,* all under general head "For Christian Friends" and in John's editing they became simply fellowship hymns. The one we still have illustrates this adaptation and use — *Thou God of Truth and Love.* Charles had written:

Didst thou not make us one
   That both might one remain,
Together travel on,
   And bear each other's pain,
Till both thine utmost goodness prove,
And rise renewed in perfect love?

Surely thou didst unite
   Our kindred spirits here
That both hereafter might
   Before thy throne appear,
Meet at the marriage of the Lamb,
And all thy glorious love proclaim. (*HP* 374)

Hymns and Psalms rightly puts this among its hymns on "MARRIAGE AND FAMILY LIFE",[3] but minus the 'marriage of the Lamb' verse, and still in John's altered form —'we' and 'all' for Charles's 'both'. It is in consequence still used mainly as a general fellowship hymn, though Methodists do now seem to be taking the hint from its placement in their new hymn-book.[4] John included seven of these Courtship hymns (*WH* 472, 475, 482, 496, 498-500). But they had first been verses about Charles's shared hopes and aspirations in marriage:

> Let us both together rise
> > To thy glorious life restored.
> Here regain our paradise,
> > Here prepare to meet our Lord.
> Here enjoy the earnest given,
> Travel hand in hand to heaven. (*WH* 498).[5]

But Wesley's hymns of relationship reach beyond family and Christian friends to community. It is Christian and right they should, but we must not be surprised to find some of them limited by the social values of those times. Especially, his philanthropy dates significantly:

> Thy mind throughout my life be shown,
> > While, listening to the wretch's[6] cry,
> The widow's and the orphan's groan,
> > On mercy's wings I swiftly fly,
> The poor and helpless to relieve,
> My life, my all, for them to give. (*HP* 318)

It is surprising that this (even with 'sufferer' for 'wretch') should have survived into the generally modern *Hymns and Psalms*. It cannot bear comparison with another hymn in that book, slightly older, but that so much better expresses the Christian conscience today:

> Thy face with reverence and with love
> > I in thy poor would see;
> O let me rather beg my bread
> > Than hold it back from thee. (*HP* 147)

But perhaps we are being rather hard on Wesley. We have already quoted with approval 'Thus may I shew' — last verse of the 'philanthropy' hymn. And better hymns of his are not mere do-gooding, but have the total Christian motivation of love:

Jesus, I fain would find
  Thy zeal for God in me,
Thy yearning pity for mankind,
  Thy burning charity;
In me thy Spirit dwell,
  In me thy mercies move;
So shall the fervour of my zeal
  Be the pure flame of love. (*HP 795*)

. . . . .

Enlarge, inflame, and fill my heart
  With boundless charity divine!
So shall I all my strength exert,
  And love them with a zeal like thine,
And lead them to thy open side,
The sheep, for whom their Shepherd died. (*HP 767*)

The gospel of the love of Jesus is the true beginning of love, and we never love our fellows more than in leading them to him. This is obscurantist only if we think the mere pious saying it is all, and not a whole new life in Christ:

Thy glory if we now intend,
O let our deed begin and end
  Complete in Jesus' name.

Freely to all ourselves we give,
Constrained by Jesu's love to live
  The servants of mankind.   (*WH* 512)

In all, there is no separating Wesley's other-worldly religion and his practical living in this world: saving one's soul and serving the present age are one verse in the original:

A charge to keep I have,
  A God to glorify,
A never-dying soul to save,
  And fit it for the sky:
To serve the present age,
  My calling to fulfil,
O may it all my powers engage
  To do my Master's will.   (*HP* 785)

The inner devotional life and living as a Christian in society are one and indivisible:

Faithful to my Lord's commands,
I still would choose the better part
Serve with careful Martha's hands
And loving Martha's heart.

Calm on tumult's wheel I sit,
'Midst busy multitudes alone,
Sweetly waiting at they feet,
Till all thy will be done.

Far above these earthly things
While yet my hands are here employed
Sees my soul the King of Kings,
And freely talks with God.   (WH 316)

. . . . .

With thee conversing, I forget
All time, and toil, and care;
Labour is rest and pain is sweet
If thou, my God, art here.[7] (HP 542)

This, again, is the story of his daily work:

Give me to bear thy easy yoke,
And every moment watch and pray,
And still to things eternal look
And hasten to thy glorious day:

For thee delightfully employ
Whate'er thy bounteous grace hath given,
And run my course with even joy,
And closely walk with thee to heaven. (HP 381)

Pattern for the Christian life is the earthly life of Christ:

Such our whole employment be,
Works of faith and charity,
Works of love on man bestowed,
Secret intercourse with God.

Vessels, instruments of grace,
Pass we thus our happy days
'Twixt the mount and multitude,
Doing or receiving good. (MHB 598)

That last line says it all. The Christian does good, having received good. It is the evangelical basis to Christian living — by God, to his sole glory:

> O let our faith and love abound!
> O let our lives to all around
>   With purest lustre shine!
> That all, but us, our works may see,
> And give the glory, Lord, to thee,
>   The heavenly light divine. (*WH* 512)

NOTES

1. We give two examples in our final paper, and *Rep Verse* has many more.
2. In *Hymns and Sacred Poems* 1749 — solely Charles's publication.
3. In *MHB* it was *Christian Fellowship*; in *WH, For the Society Praying.*
4. *MHB* anticipated this by reference to *Marriage* section.
5. We quote in final paper verses from a courtship poem left in ms — 'From all earthly expectation'.
6. Bearing the older meaning of 'wretched; — *pitiable*, rather than *contemptible* (but still with condescending overtones).
7. It has been questioned with what reality a genuine sufferer could sing 'pain is sweet'. This is the sort of poetry that is possibly not for congregational use, but that can be profound on the lips of a saint. *HP* reconstruction on basis of *Mt* 11:30 may establish itself.

14. THE OTHER WESLEY

The poetry Charles Wesley might have written if he had not been an evangelical Christian is anybody's speculation. It might not have amounted to much. As it is, all his substantial writing is evangelical. What else he wrote is both less and of much less importance. There is slender evidence of exceptional gifts beyond his capacity to write hymns. He surely could have developed clever writing, in the style of Swift. Such was his anti-Calvinist polemic, his sardonic wit fully exercised against an assured position. Like this from "The Horrible Decree', already quoted (Paper 9):

> He offers grace to all
> Which most cannot embrace,
> Mocked with an ineffectual call
> And insufficient grace. (*Works* iii, p 35; *Rep. Verse* 117)

Or from a similar diatribe:

> For fear of robbing thee
> They rob thee of thy grace,
> And (O good God!) to prove it free
> Damn almost all the race. (*Works* iii, p 83)

These are telling satire, hurling back on the Calvinists their own prime word, *grace*. But the more they are brilliant (distinct from inspired), the less they are hymns. The difference is apparent if we set against them a true and great hymn of Wesley's which says theologically the same thing, but positively, and in very different tone:

> Thy sovereign grace to all extends,
>   Immense and unconfined;
> From age to age it never ends,
>   It reaches all mankind.

> Throughout the world its breadth is known,
>   Wide as infinity,
> So wide it never passed by one,
>   Or it had passed by me.

Both are Arminian, the difference being between an opinion and an experience. It is main experience here, and the opinion is subsidiary. Wesley's position is that universal grace is the necessary corollary of experienced grace, which hence is both experimentally and logically prior. The whole hymn is evangelical testimony, with the Arminian inference embedded:

121

What shall I do my God to love,
   My loving God to praise,
The length, and breadth, and height to prove
   And depth of sovereign grace!

Thy sovereign grace to all extends ...
   Or it had passed by me.

My trespass is grown up to heaven,
   But, for above the skies,
In Christ abundantly forgiven,
   I see thy mercies rise. (*HP* 46)

All this is not principally argument, and the argument it does carry is from experience, a moving expression of evangelical religion; whereas the other was main argument, theory, the logic of it in devastating *reductio ad absurdum,* his sincere persuasion but still only an intellectual exposé of a rival evangelical belief. The hymn could only have been written by a converted man, the satires need not have been.

   Another area of controversy was the ecclesiastical, and it came to a head with his brother's presumption to ordain:

W_____ himself and friends betrays,
   By his good sense forsook,
While suddenly his hands he lays
   On the hot head of C_____ (*Rep Verse* 325)

. . . . .

So easily are bishops made
   By man's, or woman's whim?
W_____ his hands on C_____ hath laid,
   But who laid hands on him? (*Rep Verse* 326)

Whatever we think of this opinion, here is the sort of thing he writes when he is not writing hymns. His *hymns* of ministry are quite different, being about its actual practice, which seems all that concerned him at the time:

Sent by my Lord, on you I call,
The invitation is to all;
Come all the world, come, sinner, thou,
All things in Christ are ready now. (*HP* 460)

. . . . .

122

They seek him, and find, They ask and receive
The Friend of mankind, Who bids them believe;
On Jesus they venture, His gifts they embrace,
And *forcibly* enter His kingdom of grace. *(MHB 329)*

This last was 'After Preaching to the Newcastle Colliers', and the first
envisages, or may well recall, a like situation. It is hard to think Church
order was in mind when he wrote either — unless impliedly in the latter is the
thought that this has sometimes to be set aside, while the unchurched press into
the kingdom[1]. Does *forcibly*[2] mean that? — on occasion a coach and horses
through these things! Not that we are to underestimate Wesley's high-church-
manship. What he did in evangelism he did as a minister of the Church, and
he would have said, if later (especially much later) asked, that 'sent by my
Lord' was in the first place when he was ordained by a bishop. His scruple
over John's irregularity must be taken as his official and prevailing view.
There remains the difference between an ecclesiastical principle, devoutly
held, and the religious passion of actual evangelistic preaching and the
response to it. The satires are in another world of experience from the field-
preaching and the hymns that came out of it. Compare also:

Who won for God the wandering souls of men,
    Subjecting multitudes to Christ's command,
He shuts his eyes and scatters them again.
    And spreads a thousands Sects throughout the land. *(Rep Verse 327)*

and:

Enlarge, inflame, and fill my heart
    With boundless charity divine;
So shall I all my strength exert,
    And love them with a zeal like thine,
And lead them to thy open side,
The sheep, for whom their Shepherd died. *(HP 767)*

The subject is the same — the wandering souls of men, the sheep. But the
whole spirit of the hymn is different from the satire.

To his Arminian and high-church views we may add Wesley's Tory,
loyalist politics. This, for instance, on the repeated election, and expulsion
each time, of John Wilkes, left-wing libertine, as member for Middlesex:

Voters of Middlesex, forbear
    O'er your rejected Friend to grieve,
And find a Candidate as rare,
    As meet a Representative:
Beggars ye soon can qualify,
    Can Patriots from the gallows fetch;
Since then the Court Jack Wilkes sets by,
    Assert your right and chuse Jack Ketch! *(Rep Verse 283)*

It is a rather heavy humour, but Ketch, cleverly introduced to bring the two Jacks together, and with a brilliant rhyme, makes it — Ketch, a hangman of lingering ill-repute from the previous century. Or this, on the Commons' insistence, against the King's views, to negotiate peace with the American rebels, 1782:

> The doctrine is old, and obsolete too,
> That subjects should render to Cesar his due;
> The things which are his are his own proper right,
> But right must give way to oppression and might:
> Prescription and laws, constitution and charters,
> Are all swallowed up by an army of Tarters,
> Who have conquered the nation, the mob, and the House,
> So for Country and King they care not a louse. (*Rep Verse* 312)

The worst feature of these political satires is their underlying disparagement of the people. And the second is not even witty. But they must be read in the light of the current situation and events, and social ideas then. They do not show his true concern for his fellows, but his hymns show the real Wesley:

> Jesus, I fain would find
> Thy zeal for God in me,
> Thy yearning pity for mankind,
> Thy burning charity. (*HP* 795)

Such words are still modern. The others remain only as curiosities.

Altogether, the satires are in defence of three main opinions — Arminian, high-church, Tory; though we may perhaps distinguish the first from the other two. Wesley's passionate anti-Calvinism does belong in the passion of his evangelical faith. That is the one motivation, through all the tones of controversy. The hymns are there along with the satires — *Would Jesus have the sinner die? Let earth and heaven agree,* and others in the same two pamphlets of propaganda verse. The ecclesiastical and political satires are different — for all their strong feeling, they have none of the evangelical passion of the hymns. They date principally from his later life, when he was not writing quite so many hymns.

Beyond hymns and satires, Wesley has nothing that need detain us. A few compositions in contemporary style[3] he had better have left to Pope its master — longish poems in heroic couplets, sincere, but without fundamental passion, and then not lightened by anything like Pope's wit (or his own). It is surely significant that he seems never to have written hymns proper in iambic 10s, or certainly none that has been remembered.[4] He must have felt differently when he used Pope's measure. On any telling he could only have been a lyrical poet — outside of singable metres he is nothing. His miscellaneous poems in various metres, mostly about current affairs and family, take lyric form the more they take the shape of hymns — this on his courtship you could call a hymn of private devotion, if such there be:

From all earthly expectation
    Set me free,
    Seize for thee
All my strength of passion.

Keep me from thy loveliest creature
    Till I prove
    Jesus' love
Infinitely sweeter. (*Rep Verse* 238)

It is poetry — because essentially hymn.

The truth is, Wesley's greatest writing, indeed all he wrote that is of account, is unambiguously hymns — *Christ whose glory fills the skies, Jesu, lover of my soul, WRESTLING JACOB, Thou Shepherd of Israel, Lo! he comes*, poetry of that transcendent quality. These are what he really has to say, and he has frankly little else to say, and does not need to have.

NOTES

1. Just such a situation concerned not Charles but his brother, who, 'having been all my life (till very lately) so tenacious of every point relating to decency and order, that I should have thought the saving of souls almost a sin, if it had not been done in a church' (*Journal,* 31 3 39), 'submitted to be more vile' (Apr.2) in preaching to the Kingswood colliers on Hanham Mount.
2. His italics. Luke's version (16:16) of an enigmatic Gospel saying: 'the kingdom of God is preached, and every man presseth into it' ('forces a way in' — *REB*).
3. Like his eight 'Epistles' (Pope's word), of which *Rep Verse* gives two (256/7).
4. Baker gives one example of what comes near to being a hymn in such metre, out of many that do not — *Rep. Verse* 147, an undistinguished single verse, that he classifies only as a sacred poem.